TBG Publishing LLC, P.O. Box 861900, Plano, Texas 75086-1900

This publication is designed to provide accurate and authoritative information in regard to the subject matter covered. It is sold with the understanding that the publisher is not engaged in rendering professional services. If professional advice or other expert assistance is required, the services of a competent professional should be sought.

Library of Congress Control Number: 2012935026

TBG Publishing LLC

       Financial Advisor Due Diligence:
       Seeing Through the Smoke and Mirrors / by Dana Barfield.

ISBN 978-0-9771132-4-8

Printed in the United States of America

10 9 8 7 6 5 4 3 2 1

For everyone who has worked to accumulate some capital…
and wants the money to work as hard for them as they did to accumulate the money.

Financial Advisor Due Diligence:
Seeing Through the Smoke and Mirrors

By: Dana Barfield, CFP®, ChFC, MSFS

Table of Contents

Prologue

"Diligence is the mother of good fortune."
- Benjamin Disraeli

On Sunday evening, March 1, 2009, Harry Markopolos' interview on 60 Minutes finished and my mind was racing.

He is the man whose employer had asked him to investigate Bernard Madoff's investment results. Years before, Mr. Markopolos had determined Madoff's outstanding investment performance was impossible. Based on what Madoff said of his "remarkable" strategy, the amount of money he disclosed as being under his management and the stock exchange records of trading volume in the securities Madoff bought and sold, Markopolos knew something was wrong.

In the interview with Steve Kroft, Mr. Markopolos laid out in full detail how he uncovered Madoff's Ponzi scheme and how, for years, he had repeatedly requested of/pled with financial regulators to do something about it – before it was too late. The fact Markopolos was on television made clear the time for action which could have salvaged anything from the wreckage was well past.

Stories of investor suicides, bankruptcy, and heartbreak not only filled the front pages of the financial press, but also the mainstream media outlets. Madoff had promised and reported to each of his clients, year after year, that everything was perfect: their fortunes were intact, their lives were secure, and their legacies would perpetuate. Then the truth came out. It's enough to learn horribly bad news when you suspect or anticipate something is up, but when you have been led to believe things are not only good, but outstanding, it is doubly devastating.

The first thing I thought of as the interview concluded was I wanted to know Harry Markopolos better. So I reached out to him with a request for relationship on LinkedIn. To my surprise, he accepted.

Some time, perhaps a couple weeks, went by, and I continued to think about Markopolos (and Madoff). The list of Madoff's clients became public. Pages and pages, even in the smallest font, of people who lost everything they entrusted to good ol' Bernie. For many, the money they had invested was all the capital they had – every penny – now all gone.

The way my mind works, I began to wonder what an average investor, a business owner, an executive, a widow, or a retiree could do to prevent being swindled by Madoff. He had an impeccable reputation as a member of all the right country clubs, he was highly regarded in Wall Street's self-regulatory agency (NASD, now FINRA), he was a mover and shaker in Jewish philanthropy, and he absolutely looked the part.

Again, I reached out to Markopolos and asked him the following two questions:

"Is there a way someone, an average investor, could have protected himself against Madoff?"

"How would investors identify him (or others like him) and protect their money before it was too late?"

There was no answer on the other end. Just silence.

About five years earlier, I was in Scott Burns' office at the Dallas Morning News. Burns writes a financial column for several publications including Dallas' daily newspaper. Towards the end of our meeting, he congratulated me on our principled approach, personal business convictions, and the benefits we produce for our clients. Then he asked me, "How does someone – the average investor – how does he or she find you, or someone like you?"

I had no answer. Just silence.

Who Should Read This?

There are a handful of excellent books chronicling the events causing and surrounding the financial crisis which occurred during 2007-2009. There are two or three books which have detailed the various financial booms and busts over the last 150 years. I've read most of them as part of my personal "continuing education program." This book teaches you specifically how to avoid these obstacles so you can invest with the greatest likelihood of lasting success. It answers two questions: "What are the specific problems which impact my investments?" And "Personally, what do I do about them?"

This book is for the person who can control his/her spending (if you are unable to live within your means and save money without being forced to do so – this book is absolutely NOT for you). The intended reader is someone who has already accumulated some capital as a result of personal savings, retirement savings, business ownership, or inheritance. The person truly understanding and appreciating what is contained here will likely have some experience with investment advisors and, typically, some or all of that experience will be less than optimal. You might be feeling some pressure over your investments based on your age, health, family circumstances, work situation or business timeline. You likely have some combination of no desire, no expertise, and/or no time to manage your own investments, and you need someone to effectively and professionally manage your funds for you. Add in, on top of this, the last decade where so many show little or no rate of return, or worse, which you may have experienced personally or certainly know someone who has.

Throughout my career it has become clear, painfully clear for some investors, that the standard ways of meeting, interviewing, and engaging investment advisors is fraught with danger. Personal referrals are frequently based more on personality than on solid information. You end up taking the word of someone who has a good relationship with an advisor, based on criteria which could be completely unrelated to obtaining sound financial advice.

Maybe the advisor sends out holiday baskets or expensive gifts (I know one financial advisor who used to send out Calphalon cookware each year). Maybe the advisor is a fellow club member. Maybe there is some sort of "you scratch my back and I'll scratch yours" arrangement – even though these are generally illegal for investment advisors to engage in. Moreover, what makes for an outstanding investment advisor or financial planner isn't always the same as what makes one likeable – a fact far too many people learned in the market meltdown of 2008-2009.

Worth Magazine used to do a "Best Financial Advisor" list. The magazine still exists, but the list doesn't; at least not in its original form. *Worth* now has a recommended list of wealth advisors, but most manage billions of dollars, meaning the advisors on their list are off limits to investors with $10 million or less to invest.

These realities are why I'm writing this book. I'm writing so you can do three things:

- Learn how to protect yourself and your net worth against intentionally corrupt people like Bernard Madoff,
- Learn how to protect yourself from truly nice people who don't know to how manage investments, and
- Find an investment advisor providing a principled approach, having personal business convictions, and possessing a system which affords the best opportunity of producing meaningful benefits for you and your family.

Experience

I'm the one writing this book because I have been uniquely prepared to do so. My early investment career was an up-close and personal journey through what not to do. I needed a job out of school during the recession in the early 80's (remember inflation and interest rates were both sky high at that time). A nice friend introduced me to a fraudulent, "economic services" firm which recommended comparably more expensive, commission-driven, life insurance policies and hyper inflated stamp portfolios based on induced fear over inflation. Stamps and coins are an unlicensed activity.

The head of the firm and his partner took in money in $5,000 increments, pocketed 95% of it, and bought "rare" stamps with the other 5%. When all this came to light, another nice friend discovered he had unknowingly enabled the firm to bilk his friends and family members out of more than $3,000,000. Because I also had another real job and because this was strictly commission, I called on one prospect for life insurance in six months – never getting a client. The fraudster was never prosecuted and the money, that which was known and that which was unknown, was never recovered.

Next, I took a non-salary position with the second nice friend, helping him attempt to clean up the fraud into which he had unwittingly led others. We got independent appraisals on the various "portfolios" seeing what, if anything, could be salvaged from the mess. It became clear, in the very early efforts and meetings, the situation could not be fixed. Inflation was rapidly being curtailed under Reagan's economic policies. My friend sought to apologize to his clients (all of whom were friends or referrals from friends, but couldn't take the strain, and he started a computer company.

Next, I went to a big national wire house investment broker. My objective and my understanding was they would teach me how to manage money. In other words, make money for clients. What I learned instead during "training" was how to cold call and give investors the pitch each profit center of the firm had given to "trainees." There was no guidance about what to use and why; just to sell. I opened maybe 30 accounts, which averaged, as I recall, less than $2,000 a piece. I was starving, I hated it, and it didn't like me.

I was recruited to Drexel Burnham with the promise they would actually train me. Perhaps they would have, except the firm came under federal scrutiny for insider trading and a whole host of other securities violations. Michael Milken, the de facto head of the firm based on his revenue production, was investigated and subsequently pled guilty to six securities violations. People were just lined up to do business with a young, untrained broker employed by a firm in the bull's eye of Rudolph Giuliani, the United States Attorney for the Southern District of New York, and the securities regulators.

Next, I went to work for a private pension manager who managed funds administered through bank trust departments. It was like a reverse *feeder fund*. You may have heard this term as it applies to Madoff and his firm. One of the ways he accumulated so much money to manage was through funds "feeding" to him. Even though the head of this private pension manager was a decent guy, when Madoff become infamous, I understood the logistics of what took place with Madoff because of this experience.

My final stop, before starting my own firm, was with a large insurance company and its "financial planning/securities" subsidiary. I finally received excellent training in financial planning. In fact, the training was so good, after leaving, I was able to earn the most comprehensive and beneficial financial industry education credential in two quarters and eight weeks (Chartered Financial Consultant). It normally takes two or three years of study. I completed the first two classes across six months, and then did the final eight classes, one a week, in the time between November 1 and New Years Day. In the years that followed, I would earn the other publicly high-regarded credential (CFP®) and a Master's Degree in Financial Planning.

By April 1, 1990, I had had enough of the financial services industry as constituted by everyone else, and I started my own firm. I knew a substantial amount about financial planning, and one whale of a lot about what not to do regarding investments. I didn't know then, but I certainly believed, there had to be a better way to do things.

Motives

There are a number of very good reasons I do things differently than the people I was exposed to more than 20 years ago. But most importantly, I believe 1) there are consequences to poor actions, 2) money is not so important to me that I am willing to obtain it by false pretense, and 3) money is not so important that I could destroy someone else's life over it. Each one of those people/firms paid a tremendous price for their approach and/or crimes. Milken went to jail. The partners of Economic Services couldn't own assets in their own names and were married to women who knew and took advantage of that fact. Each failed to deliver on their explicit or implicit promises to me, and their actions caused me then, and continue to cause me now, grief in the form of additional scrutiny from regulators and the market place.

After what will be 22 years in a few months from the time I am writing, I have been exposed to almost all facets of an industry bent on enriching itself at the unwitting expense of its clients. I have experienced October 21, 1987, the recession of the early 1990's, the collapse of the Hedge Fund LTCM (which almost destroyed the investment markets), the Tech Bubble, the Real Estate Bubble, the Sub Prime Crisis, the Recession of 2008-2009, and, as we speak, the European Debt Crisis. This education and prior experience in proximity to some of the worst offenders in history to that point, when combined with the experience running a legitimate and successful firm for the last 22 years, uniquely qualifies me to share this book with you.

Christopher Reeve spent all the years after his spinal cord injury, using his time and resources, to advance the cause of healing what inextricably altered his life. Michael J. Fox has taken a similar approach to Parkinson's research after retiring from movies and television. Job, Moses, and Joseph in the Old Testament and Stephen in the New endured intense hardship and maintained their integrity. This book is one small part of my efforts to imitate all of these examples on issues within my sphere of influence and expertise. You, my friend, are the beneficiary of this past hardship and current effort.

Chapter 2 - What is Due Diligence?

"What we hope ever to do with ease, we must learn first to do with diligence."
* - Samuel Johnson*

Most people I come in contact with in our business are looking to have their investments supply their income at some point in the future. Some will work but want the flexibility that comes with not *having* to work. Some won't be able to work. Some will be tired of working. Putting yourself in a position of "dictating to work" instead of "work dictating to you" won't fall magically from the sky – there are all kinds of oppositions, interferences, and impediments to enjoying a life of some ease.

More than any other thing, your lifetime investment results determine your future financial circumstances. This sounds so simple as to not be worth mentioning. But the simple fact in the investment business is this: many have wandered away from producing investment results to focus more on other things. This has needlessly increased the complexity of the investment process and, as a result, has diminished the prospects of anyone seeking to produce a life with some degree of ease. You're going to know better once you finish this book.

Doing due diligence is a process to 1) avoid, or at least minimize, those oppositions, interferences, and impediments to your investment success, and 2) find someone who can put your hard earned money to work productively. Due diligence is what you do to *recognize and avoid* a bad situation *before committing money* to it. Every one of Bernard Madoff's victims recognizes today they were in a bad situation, but that recognition won't restore their funds. Proper due diligence seeks protection against bad situations *beforehand*.

Most people's perceptions of due diligence fall into two categories: either they know it needs to be done but have little or no idea how to do it, or it's too time-consuming to do right. By the time you finish this book, you will know how to do your own due diligence on potential investment advisors smartly, efficiently, and effectively.

Chapter 3 - What Causes Investment Losses?

Don't gamble; take all your savings and buy some good stock and hold it till it goes up, then sell it. If it don't go up, don't buy it.
  - Will Rogers

If you are to have any hope of successfully investing through an advisor, you need to know what causes real and irrevocable investment losses. Remembering the thing which impacts your financial future to a greater degree that anything else – your investment results – puts an important onus on preventing permanent losses of capital.

If you asked a large sampling of the population, they would tell you fraud is the largest cause of investment losses. Folks like Bernard Madoff, and Alan Stanford make the news over the magnitude of their malfeasance, but these people cause an almost infinitesimally small portion of the total losses investors incur. The truth is, far more money is lost due to false assumptions, counter-productive investment strategy, "professional" inexperience, misplaced focus, impatience, ineptitude, and herd mentality, all combined with investor misunderstanding of the financial services delivery system, than from malfeasance.

The financial regulatory system cannot effectively deal with inexperience, misplaced focus, impatience, ineptitude, and the herd mentality among financial "professionals" because none of these issues/concerns/matters are illegal. That's right: the far greater component of investor losses has no one in the position of looking after it.

The financial education apparatus is weak, variable, and becoming more so as the industry educates prospective advisors, as well as prospective customers, primarily on how to buy the industry's product offerings and not how to make investor capital work productively. This all means the investor must seek out information on his/her own from qualified resources such as this book.

So, to help you understand how the financial industry house is built, we need to understand the foundation on which is it built. In the first part of this chapter we will discuss 1) some of the actions and strategies investors are counseled to take or employ, 2) the structural flaws on which these recommendations are built, and 3) the flawed responses and advice that result.

I will suggest to you here in advance this will be the longest and most challenging chapter in the book, but to get to where we need to go together, it is also the most important. When you get a basic understanding of what we will work through together here, you'll have laid the groundwork to effectively and successfully accomplish your own investment advisor due diligence.

Structural Flaws

Bad Timing

The first thing to understand is how structural flaws in the financial industry cause tragically bad decision-making. Even though bad timing is an operational flaw, bad timing comes about because of structural issues. When an investor is "sold" an investment approach or strategy which he does not understand or which makes no sense to him, he will initially have little confidence, and eventually have no confidence, in what is being done. When this happens, bad decisions cascade on of top bad decisions, one after the other, just like an avalanche barreling downhill accumulates more snow, more mass, and more velocity. At a certain point there is no stopping the mass; there is only getting out of its way, if it's not already too late.

Such is the history of investors over the last eleven (11) or twelve (12) years beginning in calendar year 2001. Prior to this, investors were told they were fools to invest in anything other than stocks. Interest rates in the prior five years were abnormally low, so bonds paid little interest and money markets the same – all while the stock market racked up annual gains above 30% from 1996 through March 2001. Projected 15% rates of annual return from stock mutual funds seemed quite conservative when compared to what had actually happened over the preceding years.

With each successive year of the bull market beginning in 1996, investors increasingly put their money in stocks with greater and greater concentrations, later and later in the market cycle. With each additional dollar added, in each month that passed, investors increased their risk of loss. This is what the industry calls *momentum investing* – buying an investment because it has already gone up (with the thinking things are now safe to venture into the market). To be successful at momentum investing, everything must go just perfectly in the government, the economy, with unemployment, internationally, and in small businesses – but it never does!

So, instead of buying low and selling high, when momentum investing, one buys high and hopes it will go higher. This is exactly like paying $10,000 over the sticker price to buy a hybrid vehicle just as gas prices begin to fall. The consequences, far more often than not, are bad, and sometimes they are really bad.

When September 11th of 2001 hit, many sold their stock holdings when the market reopened on September 17 at a significant loss to where they invested when things were go-go in the late 1990's. They took permanent losses of capital when they sold. This same scenario of selling at the bottom repeated itself in September 2008, November 2008, and March 2009 and each time investors took hits in the form of permanent losses of capital. But more importantly for many investors, their confidence became so shaken, they were reluctant to invest in anything except where there was a guarantee of no losses.

Many people, having sold at the wrong time, in legitimate fear sat out the recover years which followed, missing an opportunity to make back more money than was lost. Timing damaged these people on the front end; then damaged them again on the back. This was not the worst mistake that one could have made.

Seeing an opportunity, the insurance industry came riding over the horizon at each instance of market loss. It is important to understand the life insurance industry does some excellent things, but when it comes to unveiling new products (especially investment products), they frequently do so when sales of their bread and butter products drop. This means their new offerings are often debuted at exactly the time consumers should NOT be investing in them.

Investors who came last to the party of bull market and experienced losses when the market fell and they sold afterward, began investing in variable life insurance, variable annuities, and equity index annuities because they were told they could have all the benefit of stock market returns with none of the risks of stock investing. There is only one problem: things don't work like that even at Disneyland. One has to pay something substantial up front to spend the day at the happiest place on earth. This is just exactly how these insurance based investment products work – you pay up front and do so substantially.

You pay high commissions and fees each and every year. You pay for things you don't need but which are sold as providing the guarantee of no losses (indemnity coverage). There are fees assessed by the manager of the funds where your money is placed (on top of all the other fees mentioned before). In some cases there are limits, called "caps," on the amount of investment return you can earn. The company will guarantee a lifetime income, but in order to receive this guaranteed income you must sign over the principal balance to the insurance company. As if that weren't enough, that guaranteed income promised is somewhere between 20 to 60% less than what other properly-managed investments will pay.

1) Buys investments close to top of market:

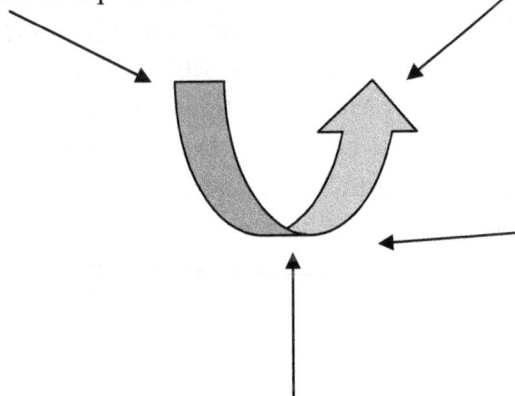

3) Recognizes insurance based investments don't keep pace and even though market has gone up, account is still stuck at the bottom (and precious time has gone by).

2) Sells investment close to the bottom of market and a) misses the recovery in fear and/or, b) buys insurance or annuities locking in losses and high expenses from which can never be recovered.

Oh, there is one more thing. Most people don't realize all of this happens…until the market recovers and their insurance-based investments don't recover. When the statements arrive saying there is no change, but the television, newspapers, and friends all show things have gone up, the insurance investor begins to suspect a problem. He investigates the possibility of leaving the investment, and he is told he certainly can do that, except there is a surrender charge somewhere between 5% and 9%, meaning a 5% and 9% fee for early withdrawal. Considering the stock losses the investor incurred by selling at or close to the bottom, then falling behind because of the insurance deal, and now a penalty for early withdrawal, he decides to just stay where he's at.

Bad-timing investment decisions follow a similar path. Investors make an otherwise reasonable investment, but do so at exactly the wrong time, and it turns out badly (sometimes disastrous). This is one of the major reasons why the average investor has struggled to earn just 3.8% rate of annual return over the last 20 years[1].

Sales Efforts v. Financial Expertise

The second thing to understand is most, in fact the *vast majority, of the people you're going to come in contact with in the financial services industry are sales people and not financial experts.* Sales people develop and manage relationships. Sales people never say no. Sales people can help you get a living trust at a good price through their referral network. Sales people might even do your taxes for you. There is no doubt that good relationships and taxes are important matters, but they have nothing to do with making sound, timely, successful investments – the kind of investments which productively put your capital to work and grow your net worth. In other words, as it applies strictly to your investing, these people add a significant layer of costs, with little or no investment benefit. This is important when you remember the thing which impacts your financial future to a greater degree than anything else are your investment results.

The sales person is the middle man in the financial services industry. These folks may have impressive initials after their names (we'll explain those a little later). They may be pillars in the community and at the club. And, while the current frustration is with compensation on Wall Street, banks, Freddie Mac and Fannie Mae, these financial sales people are the highest paid people in the industry. On a percentage basis, they make more than the CEO of BankAmerica, more than the head of trading at Goldman Sachs, and more than the head of the New York Stock Exchange combined. Because of this lucrative pay scale, their incentive is to sell you "stuff," not provide financial expertise. There is no doubt, some people overcome the incentive and act in your best interests, but the system they are in is not built to accomplish this.

Fees and Expenses

The long term rate of return on the highest returning investment in American history stands at about 9% per year today. Over the last 100 years, this is the average annual rate of return of big, blue chip stocks. The average insurance based product has an annual expense payment from the investor to the insurance company in excess of 3% - some are as high as 5% or 6%. You may say,

---

[1] Dalbar Research and Communications: Quantitative Analysis of Investor Behavior March 2011

"Oh 3 % isn't that much – a car has an 18% markup." This is true, but you don't pay a markup to the same people for the same car each and every year!

If the long term rate of return is something less than 9%, and it is after taxes, then a 3% expense ratio reduces the rate of return more than 33% each and every single year. Maybe you have mutual funds which charge a management fee (and they all do), and you're also paying the investment advisor another 1-2% for "management", you're also paying close to 3% per year. Maybe you have been referred to "professional managers" or have a wrap fee account. Typically, the total fees here exceed 2% and approach 3%.

Here is how this plays out in concrete terms: for every $100,000 invested for 25 years, the difference between 6% return and 9% return is the difference between $429,187 and $862,308 or more than double. Is it any wonder so many Americans are terribly afraid about having a successful retirement?

Taxes

Perhaps taxes are not a flaw. However, they are structural, they are an impediment, and they are reality. Taxes reduce overall investment capital and investment return. Therefore, any successful investment strategy must account for taxes. Moreover, taxes can cause flawed decision making. Most investors attempting to build a retirement today use an IRA, 401(k) or 403(b) plan for a considerable amount of their investment capital. This is understandable as there is a tax incentive to do so.

When the U.S. government was on sound financial footing, what I am about to suggest to you was unthinkable; today it is not. Investors need investments inside retirement plans for the tax benefits of accumulation and for the liability protection. However, investors also need investments not in retirement plans for the tax benefits during retirement, AND because during a financial crisis some time in the future, the biggest financial pot and the easiest access is to dollars held in government incented programs called IRA, 401(k), or 403(b) plans. Would the government ever nationalize private assets? I don't know – it would depend on the options available at the time. What I do know is there is no sense in having all your capital in retirement accounts simply because of current tax costs.

Inflation

Twenty five years ago, a loaf of bread from our Dallas area institutional bakery cost less than a dollar. Today it's almost three. If you retire at age 65, or perhaps earlier, the likelihood of living 25 years is pretty good. Just based on the bread example, you'll have to account for inflation in your investing.

Operational Flaws

Mindless Investment Management

This investment approach is a response to the issues raised earlier about high investment expenses and poor investment performance. You may have heard this called "couch potato" portfolio management. To be clear, there is no such thing as an investment portfolio you can set up once and forget (and still be successful). Moreover, there is no such thing as an investment portfolio you can set up once, then tweak once per calendar year, and still be successful either. Imagine the physician who says ignore what you eat, smoke whenever you like, refuse to exercise if you want, but just make sure you visit the doctor for an annual physical...

It is true 90% of investment managers underperform the market averages. This does not mean you cannot be successful hiring an investment manager. It just means you have to work a little harder to find one *who can* successfully manage your money. Nor does the 90% figure mean active investment management does not work: it means a lot of people picked the wrong investment manager and a lot of investment managers picked the wrong occupation. Because you have to decide whom to hire before any return is earned, you need to have a way of determining in advance whether or not someone is a good investment manager. We're going to teach you how to do just that in a later chapter.

Relying too Heavily on Statistics

Only one in five small businesses makes it more than five years. According to *the statistics*, you should never start your own business, because 80% fail within five years. When you dig deeper into the numbers, you find most small businesses start without sufficient money. You will also find most small businesses start at the wrong time in the economic cycle, just like our investor in the section on bad timing. If people rely only on *these* statistics for decision making, no one would ever start a new business.

A statistical measure relied on heavily by investment salespeople is one called Modern Portfolio Theory (MPT). Modern Portfolio Theory uses only recent, historical rate-of-return data, and nothing more, to predict which investments to purchase. In fact, MPT actually posits that it makes no difference what investments you buy (selection doesn't matter) or when you buy them (timing doesn't matter). To me, that's like having prostate cancer and saying 1) it doesn't matter that I go to an OB/GYN doctor and 2) it doesn't matter when I start treatment. But that's just me.

Most investors probably don't realize the investment recommendations (also known as asset allocations) a significant number of investment advisors provide are based squarely on these faulty theories. The way I know the theories are faulty is by talking with people who come to our office for a review of their past portfolio construction and the strategy employed in managing their investments. Discernable statistics are incredibly helpful as inputs to successful investment decision making. However, thinking sound judgment and good decision making can be replaced is asking for trouble. Unfortunately, the years 2008 and 2009 delivered exactly the kind of trouble that showed this approach to be faulty.

There is another statistically based investment approach called Technical Analysis. These days, MPT and Technical Analysis are sometimes combined in a strategy which focuses on 50 and 200 day moving averages. Even when this combined approach works fine, like when the trend of a good or bad market lasts a long time, as in 1996 to 2001, the performance is still below average at best. It can also be pretty bad if high fees are included. In choppy markets like we have had over the last three years, and are likely to have over the next several, this technique can have you buying and selling at exactly the wrong time, as discussed earlier, and this can be quite problematic. Again, statistics are no substitute for sound judgment and good decision-making, and doubling up on statistics can be, not just proportionally, but geometrically worse.

Doing What the Masses Do

When television, newspapers, and every one up and down the block is saying "buy the stocks of sub-prime mortgage brokers," it is entirely too late to do so, if it ever was a good idea to begin with. It doesn't matter whether the subject is sub-prime mortgages or blue chip stocks, if everyone is doing it, it won't work for long. By definition, when the masses are all doing the same thing at the same time, the results must be under average. Moreover, when everyone "is doing it" you're too late getting in, and when everyone is getting out, you're too late to get out. Add in expense and timing concerns and results can be disastrous.

Listening to Bankers or Governments about Investing

Here again, a decade or two ago one would never consider this an issue. But a decade ago, all bankers did was loan money to fund businesses and build homes. Today, bankers do all sorts of new things – like sell insurance products under the guise of financial "advice." Both banks and governments rely on the confidence of depositors and citizens to maintain their respective livelihoods. Without this confidence, investors stop making, and start pulling, their deposits from the banks. This is called a bank run. It is what closed down Lehman Brothers in 2008. When a government loses confidence, it can't borrow money at low rates. If the nation's debt is high like it is in many countries today, the extra interest it must pay to get investors to buy its debt can rain destruction on its economy.

As a result of this required confidence on the part of investors, bankers and government officials always believe, or at least they always say, "everything is under control" and "everything is going to work out fine." They say and do this right up until the hour things fall apart. Do not place your confidence in what you hear from these folks as it applies to your investment due diligence.

Fear or Greed Which Overruns Sound Reasoning

What prompted people to abandon their investments in the earlier bad timing example was fear. This fear was based on a lot of uncertainty… about what they actually owned in the run up, uncertainty about what makes markets run up and what makes them fall, uncertainty as to how the strategy they had "bought" would play out, uncertainty about fixing the problem, and uncertainty as to what the strategy would do next and how bad the results would be. This fear became pervasive and there was no one they knew to make sense of the situation. Fear prompted movement into insurance contracts that promised guaranteed returns, but in reality guaranteed bad results.

Craig McCann, an expert in these investments, says "Annuities are costly, complex investments sold based on typically insignificant tax or insurance benefits by financial advisors with strong financial incentives adverse to those of their customers. These financial advisors receive generous commissions for selling annuities to investors who would be far better served by investments in individual stocks and bonds or mutual funds."

He goes on to say, "We demonstrate that in most situations, investors being sold annuities will pay more taxes and have less wealth in retirement as a result of the tax treatment of investments within tax-deferred annuities. We also report the results of scientific literature which demonstrates that the death benefit feature is worth a tiny fraction of what insurance companies charge investors for this feature."

And finally, "Annuities stand out as the investment most likely to be unsuitable since in virtually every instance, the investor would have been better served by mutual fund or a portfolio of individual stocks. That variable annuities hold more than $1 trillion in assets is a testament to the powerful incentives created by the insurance industry with generous commissions and the massive fraud they engender."

Fear prompts people to do strange things. In cases referenced here, fearful investors transfer significant portions of their wealth to insurance agents and insurance companies like sheep led...well, you get the idea.

Faulty Premise

The current investment conventional wisdom embraces two strange notions: one that was once approximately true and one which is absurd. Current investment thinking bases all decisions on something called the *risk-free rate of return*. There never has been an investment with no risk, but this hasn't stopped people from basing strategy on it.

At one time, government bonds were considered risk-free because of the taxing power of each sovereign government. The full faith and credit of the United States of America once stood for something meaningful, but even this didn't make U.S. Government bonds risk-free. When interest rates rise the value of any bond declines. While holding bonds to maturity would return full principal to the bond buyer in most cases, thirty years is a long time to wait and, during this time, things change. There is a very real risk in owning bonds of any kind (and every other investment as well). No one who is paying even the slightest amount of attention today considers government bonds risk-free.

The second widely-held faulty investment premise has to do with volatility. Regular folks know this to be price fluctuation. One of the objectives of MPT is to create a portfolio of investments that earn the same amount of return every single year. Of course this sounds wonderful in theory, but in practice it is impossible. Trying to accomplish a complete absence of price fluctuation is like trying to swim to shore, against the current, with your legs tied together and your arms tied behind your back. You're going to die trying to do either of these things.

The far smarter thing to do is let the current work for you. Even in a situation where your arms and legs are bound, which I don't recommend, you have a fighting chance of making it out alive if you work with the current instead of against it. Volatility is a current you can employ as your aid, or one you can fight, struggle with, wear yourself out over, and subsequently drown.

Think of it this way: you are in the market for a new car, and car sales are slow. An excellent car brand is offering $5,000 discounts on perfectly good cars. If you need a car, and assuming the car is truly brand new and in great shape, is now a good time to buy one? Wait! Before you answer the question, you need to understand that MPT considers this price reduction as investment risk or what MPT calls volatility. MPT considers a car selling for $45,000 inherently more risky than one selling for $50,000. Is it any wonder so many investors have the investment portfolios they do?

Flawed Strategy

As we said earlier, MPT or Modern Portfolio Theory, is exclusively a statistical analysis of only one number – recent rate of return. It does no investigation of any kind into why or how the rate of return was earned. It doesn't analyze, contemplate, explore, consider, or otherwise review the economy, interest rates, debt levels, availability of financing, government regulation, market fear or hysteria, business starts, consumer confidence, unemployment, or any other reasonable, logical, or otherwise important analysis, issue, or matter – just rate of return statistics. Maybe it's just me, but this "approach" sounds a lot like a woman walking blindfolded into a hospital saying she is going to come out with a husband. She might get a sharp-dressed man who is there visiting his aging, wealthy, and generous mother. Then again she might not. I'm guessing there are many more outcomes of an undesirable nature in this scenario…and so it goes with MPT.

Another thing you may have heard is a little saying that goes like this: "It's not timing the market; it's *time in the market*." What this suggests is that you always need to have your money invested in the stock market if you are to get the best return. Surprisingly, the stock market and the prices of individual investments rise on far fewer days each year than prices fall or stay the same. And prices change favorably most frequently in short bursts.

I am in no way suggesting a strategy of constant trading in and out of investments. But what I am asking is: if prices tend to move quickly and briefly, what logic, as it relates to price alone can there be for always being in the market?

Upon examination, MPT seems to protect people from gains instead of protecting them from losses. As an investor, I suspect your hope and expectation is that it would be the other way around. This does point out that substantial losses are often caused before one penny is ever invested. It also demonstrates losses frequently have nothing to do with malfeasance. And, non-criminal losses are more widespread and often more devastating.

Flawed Response

All of this leads to a variety of responses in times of trouble, which only makes things worse. Perhaps you've heard some of these before:

- *No one knows when a recovery will occur.* There certainly are times when good advisors are caught by surprise. However, by the time the "recovery begins," substantial investment gains have been missed. The recession wasn't officially over until September of 2009, but investment gains began on March 9 of that year. This is because the market is a leading and not a coincidental or lagging indicator of the economy. If you waited to reinvest or re-enter the market until the recovery actually began, you missed substantial low-risk rates of return.

- *Your portfolio has an appropriate allocation to fixed income.* This sounds completely logical on its face - unless interest rates are at zero like they are as I write. Based on the size of the U.S. debt, there will come a time when rates rise and fixed income will encounter substantial losses based on the size and intensity of the rate increase which occurs.

- *Converting your entire portfolio to cash will guarantee you a low rate of return on your investments.* Yes it will. But in certain times the issue is not the rate of return on your capital; it is the simple *return of your capital.* Moreover, in times of deflation, cash is the more appropriate place to put your money. You then invest when prices have stopped falling – remember our earlier car purchase example?

- *If your long term goals and plans have not changed, there is no reason to change your investment strategy now.* I apologize for my anger over this one, but that is the stupidest thing I think I have ever heard. Suppose you are on I-70, west of Denver, on your way to a family ski vacation. As you approach the Eisenhower Tunnel, you discover the road is completely blocked by massive rocks which have somehow fallen from above. Since your goal of getting to Vail Mountain Ski Resort has not changed since you left Denver's airport just a little while ago, you keep your foot on the gas and drive straight into the huge boulders.

- *During a period of volatility, it is helpful to reduce the withdrawals from your portfolio.* I remember a line from the movie *Fletch* starring Chevy Chase. No worries, "I'm just foolishly spending my money on food and rent." Your financial advisor should work to have you and your investments prepared to meet your needs under the circumstances. To say after the fact, you need to reduce your withdrawals is the second stupidest thing I think I've heard.

- *Never sell investments in a down market.* The investment markets did just fine early in 2008. Bear Stearns was allowed to fail before the summer of that year. Lehman Brothers failed in September, and the markets reacted very negatively to the news, reaching a low on November 20, 2008 and another low on March 9, 2009. While there are times and situations where you should not sell investments when markets are troubled, making a blanket statement one *should never sell in bad times* is completely foolish. Nortel, General Motors, and CIT Group all filed for bankruptcy during 2009. They were troubled companies during the 2008 meltdown. If one had sold these stocks, recognizing the future was even bleaker than the present, some capital would have been preserved. Here is the point: When you discover a company is broken, you sell it to protect whatever capital you can. If the business is fine and will be fine on the other end of the trouble, the situation is not so clear cut. But when an investment is determined to truly be troubled, that investment needs to be sold to get as much of your money as possible, without regard for what the overall markets are doing.

There is a reason these recommendations are so preposterous. The one making them is trying to hold onto an income stream of back door commissions he gets paid while you remain a client (and fully invested). The fact your portfolio is decimated and you are unhappy, well… There is a reason why so many financial planners have filed for bankruptcy, gone out of business, or scaled back their operations in the last two years. Their approach (communicated as sound and effective) led to their clients losing money.

The true financial advisor's job is to try and anticipate what is going to happen, then seek to prepare you and your portfolio accordingly. No one does this perfectly, but it is far better to be approximately right than absolutely wrong. MPT and the decisions it directs have proven to be absolutely wrong. MPT starts by looking backwards, and it ends with looking backwards. If you drive an 18 wheel semi-truck for a living, then you better know how to drive with the rear view mirror. But when it comes to investing, success comes from anticipating what will happen in the future. Instead of investing with the rear view mirror, why don't we seek to prepare for what's ahead?

Chapter 4 - Critical Differences Between Salespeople and Advisors

"I observe the physician with the same diligence as the disease."
- John Donne

We've said it several times: the thing that has the greatest impact, and is the most important factor in your investing and your financial future, is your investment results. We also said earlier: 90% of investment managers, and likely an even larger percentage of financial planners, don't produce beneficial results. In fact, most planners, who are supposed to improve your outcomes, actually reduce the likelihood that your investment performance will be even just good. This is because of 1) their strong reliance on MPT, and 2) the expenses and fees they charge (those you know about) or collect (those you don't know about) all reduce the rate of return you earn. The higher these costs are, the lower your rate of return.

One of the important factors in getting excellent investment advice is the business model of the firm/person you hire to work for you. It's my considered, professional opinion if you get this first thing right, you improve the likelihood you'll get good investment results by 50%. This is not infallible, so you're still going to have due diligence work to do. But you increase your odds of success significantly in this first step alone.

What you're seeking in an investment professional is truly objective advice. After the crash of 2008 and 2009, most everyone in the financial industry is attempting to appear to be an objective advisor. This has made it more difficult to distinguish between objective advisors and those who are financial salespeople. This is compounded by the fact both salespeople and advisors can have the same initials after, and titles under, their names.

The Certified Financial Planner® professional program is a widely known designation. There are some easy delineators of salespeople and advisors, but CFP® is not one of them. This is no knock on the CFP® program, as I will explain in a later chapter. It's just that those earning the CFP® certificate can be salespeople or advisors. I'm going to teach you how to know the difference.

Financial salespeople are either securities brokers or insurance agents. However, neither of these people use these titles in describing or identifying themselves. Brokers are employed by broker-dealers, which sometimes go by the name of "investment bankers." Insurance agents are employed by, or representatives of, insurance companies or insurance agencies. But here again, neither broker-dealers nor insurance agencies are using these identifiers.

These firms are widely known financial salespeople which operate to some degree as broker-dealers:

Ameriprise	Dain Rauscher
Charles Schwab	Edward Jones

Fidelity Investments
Goldman Sachs
LPL
Merrill Lynch
Miller Tabak Roberts
Raymond James

Scottrade
Smith Barney
Southwest Securities
Stiefel Nicholas
UBS (formerly Paine Webber)

These are widely recognized insurance companies which are financial salespeople:

AFLAC
Genworth
Lincoln National
Mass Mutual
Met Life
New York Life

Northwestern Mutual
Pacific Life
Principle Financial
Prudential
TIAA-CREF
Transamerica

Certainly, some of the people at these broker-dealers and insurance companies do good work. You just need to know these firms are financial salespeople, making their money as a result of the products they are able to sell you. Whether those products are in your best interests or not, their financial incentives are to sell products.

Many of these firms also own or have registered investment advisor subsidiaries or divisions. This does not change the fact that the majority of each firm's revenue comes from life insurance and investment sales – not advice. I show details of one example in the next chapter.

Salespeople Specifics

The 1983 movie *Trading Places*, starring Eddie Murphy, Dan Aykroyd, and Jamie Lee Curtis provides an outstanding understanding of a "financial salesperson" (called a broker in this movie).

In the movie, Ralph Bellamy and Don Ameche play the owners of a commodities brokerage firm named "Duke and Duke." To fill their time, Randolph and Mortimer Duke decide to run a little social science experiment: they frame the president of their firm as a drug dealer rendering him homeless (Aykroyd as Louis Winthorpe). They locate a homeless drug dealer and make him the president of their firm (Murphy as William Valentine).

After the transfer of position takes place, Randolph and Mortimer are explaining the brokerage business to Valentine, "Some of our clients want to buy commodities, and some of our clients want to sell commodities. Whether our clients buy or sell doesn't matter, because either way, Duke and Duke gets a commission. Do you understand William?"

"Yea…sounds to me like ya'lls a coupla bookies," says Valentine immediately.

"See Mortimer, I told you he would understand," explains Randolph.

William Valentine accurately characterizes brokers as book makers – those who don't care which team wins, but who benefit from the spread and the vigorish. The same things apply to investing. The spread is the difference between the bid and the ask, or what they have to pay versus what they can sell for. Seldom is there ever a situation where there is no spread. And the vigorish is the commission, or the price of doing business.

You now know all you need to know about any sort of broker. They make money buying things from one group while simultaneously selling the exact same things to another group. Brokers don't care whether the value of anything goes up or down. They don't provide true objective advice. They give sales pitches – sometimes smooth, compelling, and/or enticing – but nevertheless a sales pitch. What they care about is selling things.

Goldman Sachs is a huge investment bank and broker-dealer firm. Much has been made about Goldman's role in the financial crisis: how they simultaneously sold mortgage securities and bet these investments would fail. Goldman Sachs played both sides of the deal then, and they still do it today. What's more, it is perfectly legal. This is what brokers do: they sell things and make money regardless of which direction the investments go. People are up-in-arms over this practice, and there is little the authorities can do. Brokers are sales people. They play both sides of the deal, period.

The most successful employees at these broker dealers have titles like "Vice President: Investments." Pretty impressive, huh? You need to know these titles are given, not as a function of how beneficial the broker has been to his clients, but how much commission the broker has generated for the broker-dealer. Those commissions come out of your (investor's) pocket.

Salespeople in Disguise

Over the years, the number of brokers has declined as people lose money to these salespeople and go elsewhere. Enter the "financial planner", also known as a "financial advisor". The cost of hiring and training a broker is high, and most people who are hired never pan out. It takes a long time to study for the necessary exams and to get properly registered with the regulatory agencies. Plus, trainees are paid during this time, which can take months or even years.

After all of the prep work is completed, it still takes a broker significant time to build a client list that generates enough commission to pay him wages and to pay the firm back on its investment – perhaps a couple years (this is very much like trying to get a teenager off your dime and onto his or her own). Broker-dealers needed a way to get new brokers generating more revenue more quickly.

Having "financial advisors" selling mutual funds in slick presentations all based on MPT (Modern Portfolio Theory) proved to be just the ticket – for the brokers-dealers and their employees. It proved to be a disaster for investors like you, who lost trillions of dollars in the events of 2001 and 2008-2009.

The Unmistakable Mark of Financial Salespeople

The following appears on the website of a Southeastern U.S. financial advisor (in this size and type font):

Mr. [So and So] is a Wealth Advisor with such and such firm, and the Branch Manager of two [Such and Such] branch offices. As a Certified Financial Planner, CFP®, Mr. [So and So] has provided financial advice and guidance to his clients for over fifteen years.

This guy really sounds like he is something. He seems to be an objective, client-oriented, financial advisor who has been in business for 15 years. Then at the bottom of each page of the site, the following words appear, again in the same font size as depicted:

Securities and advisory services offered through LPL Financial, Member FINRA/SIPC

Securities and advisory services offered through [Such and Such], Member FINRA/SIPC[*] is the unmistakable indication this person is a financial salesperson, earning at least a portion of his income though the commissions generated from investment sales. But, this guy probably also earns income from fees for "managing assets." Interestingly enough, as I search another area of his website where the LPL Financial "advertisement" appears on his site, I find this:

Over $283 billion in assets as the broker/dealer of record***
Over $75 billion in fee based platform assets**

The top number consists primarily of the amount of financial products LPL Financial has been able to sell. The bottom number is the dollar amount on which it charges asset management fees. These numbers support the reality that LPL is primarily a broker making money selling products, while perhaps giving an appearance as an objective advisor. Furthermore, the assets considered "fee based platform assets" may be investment products they sold for commission *that also are charged an asset management fee*. This is an example of how multiple fees and expenses siphon off return from customers and place it in the hands of "salespeople."

More isn't Necessarily Better, Sometimes it's Just More

Many investment firms of all types tout how large they are and how many assets they manage. The mere fact that a firm manages a lot of assets is of no particular benefit to you. In fact, frequently the larger the firm, the greater the temptation to focus on the firm's income numbers instead of the customer's investment performance numbers.

---

[*] (If the salesperson is an employee of the firm doing the transaction(s), it might only say "Member FINRA/SIPC").

Big car companies are beneficial because of the economies of scale in buying parts, supplies, and services. Big transportation companies like Federal Express are beneficial because they can deliver packages to every corner of the earth. When it comes to investment management, there are limited opportunities for economies of scale. We don't buy or carry inventory. We don't have to go to Australia, Kenya, China, and every other country, every single day.

Firms frequently wrap themselves in the terms "worldwide" and "global reach." The truth about the investment business is, if you have a phone and a fast internet connection, you have the same tools as the largest financial firms anywhere in the world. Warren Buffett, widely recognized as the best investor of all time, ran his investment firm with only himself and a secretary for many years.

Salespeople Who Recommend Other Managers

After clients caught onto the broker in financial planner garb, firms began having their financial salespeople recommend "professional money managers." These are firms, reportedly independent from the broker-dealer, hired to manage money for the broker.

In many cases, the broker makes more money from the "finder's fee" he receives from the "professional money manager" than he would from commissions if he ran the money himself. Then the "professional money manager" charges a hefty fee on top of what the broker gets paid. As far as high fees and expenses go, this is the same song, second verse.

But there is more. It's exactly this type of arrangement which enabled and enhanced Bernard Madoff's ability to steal billions of dollars from unsuspecting investors. One of the things financial salespeople say when they recommend "professional money managers" is they (the salespeople) have run extensive due diligence on the "professional money managers." In other words, they have vetted their records, performance, and so on. My only question is this: if they really did do extensive due diligence, then how was Madoff able to steal all that money?

Salespeople Who Recommend Mutual Funds

Mutual fund is just another format for "professional money manager." There are some excellent mutual fund operators like Sequoia, Dodge and Cox, and T. Rowe Price. The difficulty with mutual funds is there isn't a way of knowing what you actually own. Once each quarter, funds provide a breakdown of their holdings, but this fund composition changes by the hour in most funds. This lack of transparency works against making informed decisions. It is also a lack of transparency which leads to many other investment pratfalls.

Frequently, financial salespeople recommend what are called proprietary funds. This is a fund owned by the same firm doing the recommending. Most proprietary funds are more expensive for investors than independent funds like the ones mentioned above, and the proprietary fund performance is almost always worse than independent peers. I'll teach you more about this subject in the next chapter.

Some financial salespeople tout themselves as mutual fund experts with credentials like CFS (Certified Fund Specialist), or CMFC® (Charter Mutual Fund Counselor). What you need to know is that the major difference between all mutual funds (called fund classes) is when, how, and how much commission the fund pays to the brokers (financial salespeople) who recommend the fund. There are no-load funds which pay no upfront commissions. There are load funds which pay upfront commissions. There are back-end loaded funds which pay a commission to the broker immediately, but hold the investor hostage with a surrender charge when they try to exit. Every other fund class is essentially a derivation or modification of these three possibilities.

Other Financial Salesperson Incentives

We have seen financial salespeople have profound incentives counter to the interests of you, the investor and client. Some salespeople are able to reduce the priority of those incentives and perform well for clients. But many, perhaps most, these days cannot and do not place their own interests behind the interests of those seeking expertise and advice.

On top of the incentives we've already discussed, there are others. Most insurance salespeople are contractually obligated to place the interests of the insurance company ahead of the client. This is one reason why we do no insurance-based investments. Our clients come to us to protect their interests. Insurance companies have fleets of attorneys to protect their interests. My job as an investment advisor is to look out for my clients.

Many insurance agencies receive office cost reimbursements. They can win sales contests and prizes based on commissions produced. These inducements are based on hitting certain sales revenue (commission) targets. If an insurance company pays a firm an office reimbursement for hitting sales goals, what products do you think the firm will recommend?

Salespeople Endorsed By Others

It is illegal for a true investment advisor to be endorsed by a media personality, trade organization, celebrity, or business. This means a "financial advisor" who receives any endorsement is a salesperson and not an advisor.

It is somewhat common for trade groups to endorse someone in the financial business because the one endorsed then offers an insurance, or other, discount to membership. A friend of mine is an executive at a national insurance company that sells insurance *only through these endorsements*. Typically, the programs offer discounts for workers comp, disability, or property and casualty insurance. These programs are often good for all involved.

There is a well known financial media person who endorses financial advisors calling them "endorsed local providers." The last question on his "financial advisor" signup form is: "Do you carry the designation of Registered Investment Advisor (RIA) or Investment Advisor Representative (IAR)?" The reason for this is true financial advisors cannot be endorsed and therefore are not eligible for his program.

Those who refer or endorse can easily give legitimate due diligence a passing glance. Looking back to the heading of the signup form identifies this organization's priorities for the ones they endorse: "...certain standards for participation, such as being an established professional and having a process in place to quickly follow up with our referrals." If I were an investor looking for a good advisor, I would be glad to accept prompt follow-up, but even more than that, I want true expertise instead of the potential for a sales pitch.

From the standpoint of budgeting, debt philosophy, controlling money instead of money controlling you, efficient use of resources, and self control, Dave Ramsey gives excellent advice. I have read and benefitted from his work. We also recommend his materials on these subjects to others. But based on the law, his company's endorsement of people in the financial business necessarily omits many of the highly qualified people who can help you with your investments. Based on his screening, he knows this but there is precious little he can do about it.

Institutional vs Retail Operations at Investment Banks

Big investment banks have institutional and retail operations. The institutional side of the business deals with hedge funds, investment advisors, insurance companies, mutual funds, and so forth. These clients generate huge amounts of revenue for these investment banks and, as such, get first crack at whatever beneficial deals that bank does.

The retail side of the business is for individual investors. Generally speaking, the largest retail client generates substantially less in commissions than the smallest institutional client. Even so, the retail side generates substantial revenue for the firm. Moreover, the retail side of the operation provides an additional source of people to sell less desirable deals.

The Most Important Reason You Need a Financial Advisor

Anyone can be a "financial expert" when the markets are hospitable and going up every day like they did from 1996-2000 and from 2003-2008. It's when the pressure is on, when things are choppy or worse, that you need expert assistance. This is completely counter to the job description, and to the day-to-day operation of a financial salesperson. Sales people in the financial business are what management likes to think of as "asset gatherers." The job of asset gatherers is to seek new relationships, new sources of cash from old relationships, and to bring those assets into the firm (just like we saw earlier with the North Carolina guy). There is no training of any substantial nature provided in the financial sales "system" for how to deal with trouble. And there is a reason for that – there's no short-term incentive to do so.

Most financial salespeople bring in healthy amounts of new assets when times are good. When times are bad, new assets are not necessarily needed to generate significant commission revenue. Remember, the brokerage firms generate commissions when you buy and when you sell – they don't care which you do. So, when things start going poorly, most clients of financial sales people have not sold. Trouble starts, and then some clients sell. Trouble continues, and more clients sell. Trouble reaches its ultimate trough and the rest of the salesperson's clients sell right at the bottom. With each sale, a commission is generated for the broker and firm, AND with each sale comes an opportunity to sell something else, which generates another commission for the broker and firm.

In the 80's and 90's, the financial sales industry determined that 50% or more of the firm's future revenue would come from brokers and customers it didn't currently know. The industry's response was to constantly hire new brokers, push them to add new clients, squeeze as much revenue as possible from the "relationship," and then hire more brokers. This short term thinking still pervades the financial sales industry today. This is a big reason why so many investors have such poor investment results, not just for the last few years, but for the last decade or more. Helping clients mange their funds when the pressure is on runs counter to the job the broker was hired to do – gather assets.

With all of these headwinds in the "system," it's no wonder investor results are so poor. You've got to get out of this pit. In the next section, we look at what a legitimate financial expert "looks like."

Specifics of True Investment Advisors

Like many other first generation investment advisors, I came out of the brokerage/financial sales person model. As I explained at the outset of this book, and as you have read in the subsequent chapters, I can point out most of the land mines. I have said for the last 22 years that I left that business because of the inherent conflicts of interest between the brokers/firms and the clients. In that business, it is possible for the brokers/firms to make tremendous amounts of money, while the client makes none or loses his, which sounds just like Valentine's characterization, "Ya'lls a coupla bookies."

1) I hated that situation. 2) I was a complete failure in it. 3) I could not take advantage of people for the sole purpose of making money myself. Was it some magic or goody-two-shoes upbringing which produced this in me and other successful managers? No, it was being forced to work.

"Being forced to work, and forced to do your best, will breed in you temperance and self-control, diligence and strength of will, cheerfulness and content, and a hundred virtues which the idle will never know."
- Charles Kingsley

A person who has been forced to work to get ahead makes the best financial advisor. Warren Buffett's parents never gave him a dime. The billions he has made investing all started with his own work. He bought cokes in six packs from his family grocery store and sold them in the neighborhood at a single serving price. This is what 7-Eleven does to this very day. David Einhorn started his hedge fund with a very small amount of money he raised on his own and built the fund into a powerhouse. Kyle Bass started with only the money he earned from years of work. The list goes on and on.

Requirements for Financial Advisors

A true financial advisor, someone who is a financial expert capable of assisting you, is a fiduciary. True fiduciaries have the legal obligation to do what is in the best interests of the people they represent. No excuses, no ifs, ands, or buts.

As an aside, there are some people considered fiduciaries who have potentially compromised themselves, but we'll discuss that in the next chapter on "disclosures."

A fiduciary has the responsibly to disclose where their interests conflict with the interests of clients. Does the fiduciary receive inducements which sway the advice they give and the decisions they make (we saw clear examples on this earlier)? Does the fiduciary benefit financially or otherwise at times different than the client does? What decisions and under what circumstances does the advisor's interest take precedence over the client's?

Any time an advisor/firm is enriched or benefited in a way or at a time the client is not, there is a conflict of interest. In my firm, we make more money only when our client's account balances go up and we make less money when those balances go down. My firm does not receive, earn, or accept any commissions or incentive payments on the investments we manage – zero. My firm's fortunes are inextricably linked to the success of our clients, period. This is the fiduciary standard and it is what you should expect from your advisor.

You should expect full and complete disclosure of compensation the firm earns, fees and expenses your account incurs, and any other charges, which in some way are deducted from your account or otherwise reduce your investment performance. Every investment purchase and every financial transaction has some sort of cost attached to it. Either the yield earned is lower because of the costs/charges (like on a certificate of deposit), or there is a direct cost (like when buying a stock).

Reality of a Good Advisor

Our clients pay a small commission on what we invest in but neither my firm nor I, get even a penny of that. These commission charges come out of the account, and even though the charges are small, this expense reduces the account balance. Accordingly, each commission charged to our client's account reduces the amount of money my firm earns. This creates a mutual interest for our client and for our firm to keep commission charges as low as possible - commissions cost both of us money at the same time and in the same proportion to each other.

This incentive, which is built into every one of our client relationships, aligns my interests, those of my firm, and those of our client. Each of us benefits at the same time and in the same proportion as the other. These arrangements are what you are seeking when you retain investment advice.

You really want an investment firm which is privately owned by the people giving the investment advice. When most businesses go public the effect is benign, but in the investment business being public grants the ability to use someone else's capital. *This provides extra incentive to take risk* because the firm is doing so with shareholder capital instead of its own money. This puts your (the investor's) money at greater risk. This fact enabled and accelerated Lehman Brothers' demise.

Active owners of private firms are utilizing their own capital, risking their own financial livelihoods, and putting their own reputations on the line. These risks they take with their own funds reduce the risks you will take as a result of their management. Moreover, an independent advisor who has been in business for the last ten years or more (before 2006 or so), and who earns no commissions on the investments he manages, is still in business because their financial management has been effective. Otherwise, it is likely he wouldn't survive given the risks and costs. This is what you are now seeking: effective financial management.

Responsibilities of a Good Advisor

Here is the investment advisor's actual job description. These are the things required to productively put your money to work. They are also the reasons why it is so difficult for investors, with full time jobs in something other than investing, to manage their own money.

1. Do keep money in cash sufficient to cover your expenses over 6-36 months time.

2. Don't chase yield.

3. Do invest with cash flow in mind.

4. Do come to terms with seeking capital gains as a necessity in a low interest rate environment.

5. Do invest in high quality companies when they are out of favor.

6. Don't think every penny must be invested all the time.

7. Do sit in cash, even when it earns nothing, if there are no truly outstanding bargains.

8. Do exhaustive and substantive research on what you invest in.

9. Do that research on a constant, timely, and efficient basis.

10. Do remember you are investing for results which will come in the *future*; analyze each investment accordingly.

11. Don't invest in things simply because of what has happened in the past (some investments drop in price because they are bad investments, some drop because people don't understand, some drop because people panic).

12. Do carefully track and evaluate domestic and worldwide economic issues, but...

13. Don't expect successful investments to track in lock-step with a good/bad economy.

14. Do keep your head about you when others are losing theirs – good and bad. The only way you can do this is if you truly know what is taking place, have a plan in place to deal with the existing conditions, and have experienced these, or similar, conditions before (from a practical investment context).

15. Do have a plan in place to deal with inevitable market declines, sideways markets, and excessive market increases.

16. Do remember, at any one instant in time, the value of an investment can differ materially from the price of that investment, but over time if the investment increases in value, the price of the investment does likewise.

When the first sixteen items on this list were written, our intention was to use it as an instructional piece about the things an individual must do to manage his or her own money: "the do's and don'ts of managing your own investments" was the notion. What became clear about this investment process, the one which affords the best opportunity for success, is that it requires full time work to accomplish. Therefore, here is point number seventeen…

17. Do hire a professional who is both experienced and successful in this type of investing.

Chapter 5 - The Imperfections of Advisor Disclosures

There is always a "but" in this imperfect world.
- Anne Bronte

Every company must turn a profit to stay in business, and the financial services business is no different. The concern, though, is the same as any other business where the "professional" knows far more than the client, customer, or patient and, as a result, has the ability to use that knowledge to enrich himself or herself at the expense of the client.

Hidden Disclosures

Now how is that for an oxymoron – hidden disclosure? This problem arises when industry participants hide or disguise information about conflicts, expenses, or incentives which are counter to their client's interest. Sometimes, the disclosure is hidden in plain sight.

There is a movie that is instructive in this matter also: *Class Action* (1991) starring Gene Hackman and Mary Elizabeth Mastrantonio. Father and daughter are opposing attorneys in a suit over exploding automobiles that have killed a number of people.

Hackman, as the plaintiff's lawyer, is entitled to full disclosure of every relevant piece of evidence Mastrantonio's client has. Hackman's character is looking for specific information about whether anyone knew in advance about an electrical circuit which was alleged to cause these horrific car explosions. As it turns out, such evidence existed. A company research employee discovered it and shared the information with company executives.

Customers are entitled to disclosure of *relevant* information related to the investment they are about to make. This information exists.

Mastrantonio's boss at the law firm decides to disclose ALL information, instructing literal truckloads of documents to be sent to the plaintiff's lawyer. All of the information was in plain sight, but there was such a volume of it, no one could assemble the facts in sufficient time and adequate order to identify what was important.

Customers receive (or by law are supposed to receive) a prospectus (200 pages or more is not uncommon when it comes to insurance products) which contains information about the investment they are considering. Frequently, the prospectus alone does not contain all the information needed to make an informed decision. Many times a supplement is needed. Documents the clients must sign to complete the investment can also contain additional disclosures. Sometimes other documents (such as company annual reports), not normally a part of the investment process, are needed to fully understand the investment, the promoter, or others having an impact on what could occur.

Recently a friend and his wife, who were doing business at the large financial planner AmeriPrise, approached me about reviewing some of the investments and investment arrangements which had been recommended to them. The couple didn't know exactly what was going on but began to become suspicious over all of the fees and expenses they perceived they were being charged. I agreed to do the review and learned some very interesting information about the company, which is all a matter of public record.

In a class action settlement offer dated February 15, 2007 I learned there were investor complaints where it was alleged customers "were sold financial plans and/or advice that, instead of being tailored to their individual circumstances, contained standardized recommendations designed to steer them into investing in Defendants' proprietary mutual funds and other proprietary investment products and certain non-proprietary "Preferred" or "Select" mutual funds."[2] RiverSource Investments is one of the named complainants. As it turns out RiverSource is the name of AmeriPrise' wholly owned annuity unit

Plaintiffs also allege the defendant gave "plans or advice that was tainted by inadequately disclosed conflicts of interest. Specifically, clients who purchased financial advice, financial plans, or other financial advisory services were given investment recommendations that were improperly influenced by [plaintiff's] financial interests rather than the individual needs of [clients]."[3] *That's pretty interesting*, I thought to myself. *Hmm. I wonder if there is anything to this.*

Curious, I decided to track down the 80 page RiverSource Annuity prospectus. The one I found was dated April 29, 2011. Here is what it says on page 16 (there is no need to try and read this):

Revenuewereceivefromthefundsmaycreatepotentialconflictsofinterest:Weorouraffiliatesreceivefromeachofthefunds,orthefunds'affiliates,varyinglevelsandtypesofrevenueincludingexpensepaymentsandnon-cashcompensation.
Theamountofthisrevenueandhowitiscomputedvariesbyfund,maybesignificantandmaycreatepotentialconflictsofinterest.ThegreatestamountandpercentageofrevenueweandouraffiliatesreceivecomesfromassetsallocatedtosubaccountsinvestinginthefundsthataremanagedbyouraffiliatesColumbiaManagementInvestmentAdvisers,LLC(ColumbiaManagementInvestmentAdvisers)orColumbiaWangerAssetManagement,LLC(ColumbiaWangerAssetManagement)(affiliatedfunds).EmployeecompensationandoperatinggoalsatalllevelsaretiedtothesuccessofAmeripriseFinancial,Inc.anditsaffiliates,includingus.Certainemployeesmayreceivehighercompensationandotherbenefitsbased,inpart,oncontractvaluesthatareinvestedintheaffiliatedfunds.Weorouraffiliatesreceiverevenuewhichrangesupto0.64%oftheaveragedailynetassetsinvestedintheunderlyingfundsthroughthisandothercontractsweandouraffiliateissue.Weorouraffiliatesmayalsoreceiverevenuewhichrangesupto0.04%ofaggregate,netoranticipatedsalesofunderlyingfundsthroughthisandothercontractsweandouraffiliateissue.PleaseseetheSAIforatablethatrankstheunderlyingfundsaccordingtototaldollaramountstheyandtheiraffiliatespaidusorouraffiliatesinthepriorcalendaryear.Expensepayments,non-cashcompensationandotherformsofrevenuemayinfluencerecommendationsyourinvestmentprofessionalmakesregardingwhetheryoushouldinvestinthecontract,andwhetheryoushouldallocatepurchasepaymentsorcontractvaluetoasubaccountthatinvestsinaparticularfund(see"AbouttheServiceProviders").Therevenueweorouraffiliatesreceivefromafundoritsaffiliatesisinadditiontorevenuewereceivefromthechargesyoupaywhenbuying,owningandsurrenderingthecontract

The information is so small and tightly packed on page 16 of the prospectus that this is what comes out when I attempted to copy the information from the pdf file. Here is that prospectus disclosure word for word, but reformatted.

Revenue we receive from the funds may create potential conflicts of interest: We or our affiliates receive from each of the funds, or the funds' affiliates, varying levels and types of revenue

---

[2] United States District Court, Southern District of New York, Master File No. 04 Civ 1773 (DAB)
[3] Same document

including expense payments and non-cash compensation. <u>The amount of this revenue and how it is computed varies by fund, may be significant and may create potential conflicts of interest.</u> The greatest amount and percentage of revenue we and our affiliates receive comes from assets allocated to subaccounts investing in the funds that are managed by our affiliates Columbia Management Investment Advisers, LLC (Columbia Management Investment Advisers) or Columbia Wanger Asset Management, LLC (Columbia Wanger Asset Management) (affiliated funds)."

Employee compensation and operating goals at all levels are tied to the success of Ameriprise Financial, Inc. and its affiliates, including us. Certain <u>employees may receive higher compensation and other benefits</u> based, in part, on contract values that are invested in the affiliated funds. We or our affiliates receive revenue which ranges up to 0.64% of the average daily net assets invested in the underlying funds through this and other contracts we and our affiliate issue. We or our affiliates may also receive revenue which ranges up to 0.04% of aggregate, net or anticipated sales of underlying funds through this and other contracts we and our affiliate issue. <u>Please see the SAI for a table that ranks the underlying funds according to total dollar amounts</u> they and their affiliates paid us or our affiliates in the prior calendar year.

<u>Expense payments, non-cash compensation and other forms of revenue may influence recommendations your investment professional</u> makes regarding whether you should invest in the contract, and whether you should allocate purchase payments or contract value to a subaccount that invests in a particular fund (see "About the Service Providers"). The revenue we or our affiliates receive from a fund or its affiliates is in addition to revenue we receive from the charges you pay when buying, owning and surrendering the contract.

Ameriprise sells annuities from one of their wholly owned subsidiary companies. This annuity arrangement pays Ameriprise investment professionals more commission if they recommend company-owned funds. The prospectus clearly that states the additional amount of money earned this way can be significant, and this entire arrangement creates a conflict of interest. Then, in the final paragraph, it is disclosed that Ameriprise representatives receive expense reimbursements and non-cash compensation for making recommendations of company-owned funds and this "may influence recommendations of your investment professional."

Having found this, I dug deeper and located the 290 page "Statement of Additional Information (SAI) for RiverSource Variable Annuity" dated April 29, 2011. On page 4 of this document it shows where investor money into RiverSource/Ameriprise annuities was invested for 2010.

Affiliated Funds*	$228,088,727.84	72.02%
Oppenheimer Variable Account Funds	$15,628,735.56	4.93%
Fidelity Variable Insurance Products	$14,724,257.96	4.65%
Invesco VanKampen Variable Insurance Funds	$11,870,799.94	3.75%
Janus Aspen Series	$6,582,362.41	2.08%
Alliance Bernstein Variable Products Series Fund,Inc.	$5,575,475.35	1.76%
Wells Fargo Advantage Variable Trust Funds	$5,074,972.89	1.60%
PIMCO Variable Insurance Trust	$5,059,767.06	1.60%
Franklin/Templeton Variable Insurance Products Trust	$4,281,966.04	1.35%
Eaton Vance Variable Trust	$3,798,366.80	1.20%
American Century Variable Portfolios,Inc.	$3,762,399.53	1.19%
Goldman Sachs Variable Insurance Trust	$3,644,842.55	1.15%
MFS Variable Insurance Trust SM	$2,954,011.59	0.93%
Morgan Stanley UIF	$1,888,990.85	0.60%
Putnam Variable Trust	$1,013,384.89	0.32%
Neuberger Berman Advisers Management Trust	$989,755.86	0.31%
Credit Suisse Trust	$841,648.92	0.27%
Royce Capital Fund	$330,694.17	0.10%
Third Avenue Variable Series Trust	$301,521.50	0.10%
Dreyfus Investment Portfolios Dreyfus Variable Investment Fund	$124,287.46	0.04%
Calvert Variable Series ,Inc.	$118,238.87	0.04%
Legg Mason Partners Variable Portfolios	$38,989.33	0.01%
Lazard Retirement Series,Inc.	$2,317.20	0.00%
Lincoln Variable Insurance Products Trust	$1,898.72	0.00%
J.P.Morgan Series Trust II	$1,552.86	0.00%
	$316,699,966.15	100.00%

Additional cash compensation available due to affiliate relationship (Annual)
This does not include investor deposits for all other years. $1,551,003.35

What you see in the table is more than 72% of all money that went into Ameriprise variable annuities in 2010 was invested in Ameriprise-owned (affiliated) funds. We discussed in an earlier chapter how commissions influence the recommendations of financial salespeople. Here, you have an excellent example of this reality: additional compensation potential motivates Ameriprise brokers to put 72% of all new variable annuity investment dollars into Ameriprise- owned funds. Remember these numbers are just for one year – 2010.

Forgive my sarcasm, but it sure looks like the class action lawsuit had a big impact! I was never able to determine from where the extra fee is paid – whether that is an additional charge to the client/investor, it comes out of the up-to 1.67% charge for investment fund operating expenses[4],

---

[4] Page 9 of the prospectus

44

out of the up to 1.20% mortality and expense charges,[5] or out of the maximum .25% rider charges. It is important to remember these fees are annual fees.

All of this information is disclosed in appropriate Ameriprise documents. It took me a full day to assemble and interpret the data.

Detrimental Disclosures

A second problem arises when disclosures are made which alter the fiduciary relationship a client has entered into with an advisor, thereby compromising the client's interests. In a situation where this relationship alteration takes place, the advisor intentionally stops acting as a fiduciary in order to sell high commission insurance products we discussed earlier. But, in my observation the advisor does not specifically tell the client this, nor is the matter discussed directly. If an "advisor" told his client, "You're on your own here. This is not in your best interests, but I am recommending it anyway," no one would invest in this stuff. It's no reach whatsoever to recognize the advisor seldom, if ever, has this conversation.

This "disclosure" is tucked away in a large volume of information called the prospectus. According to attorney's we've spoken to, the information in the prospectus is specifically designed to defeat the client's ability to file a claim against an advisor the client believed to be a fiduciary, when the advisor sells the client a high-commission, poorly-performing, high-expense, increased-income tax, "investment" product, the client discovers it and when the client then wants to sue.

Most people believe their financial advisor is a fiduciary – where he or she has the requirement to do what is in the client's best interest. There are some financial advisors who are fiduciaries, but sellers of annuity products, as well as all other financial salespeople, are not. Therefore, they have no obligation to do that which is in the client's best interests. Only a registered investment advisor, as described in the previous chapter, is an investment fiduciary.

The courts have found there is no fiduciary relationship between the insurance company/agent and the purchaser of the annuity. Since there is no fiduciary relationship, the broker/agent cannot breach a fiduciary duty regardless of what he/she does. The courts dismiss fraud and disclosure claims, because insruance companies have 200-page prospectus specifically stating these facts. Most investors don't read the prospectus – but all the bad stuff is in there, or at least is in there and several other documents.

Here are examples of some other disclosures financial companies make. What you will notice are the interests of the firm being placed ahead of the customer's interest, conflicts due to compensation, conflicts between customers for the same product, conflicts with parent companies, conflicts with subsidiary companies, and conflicts which cause financial sales people to favor a

---

[5] Page 10 of the prospectus

better-paying product over a potentially better-performing product. All the following statements are taken directly from the respective company's disclosure, marketing, sales, and/or employee materials posted publicly on their respective websites.

This from <u>Ameriprise Financial</u>:

Ameriprise Financial Services has promotional agreements with certain product companies. These companies may pay for training and education events, such as seminars for employees, financial advisors, clients and prospective clients, or due diligence meetings.

For employees and financial advisors, these events may be held at off-site locations and the travel, meals and accommodations may be paid for by the product company. Additionally, these companies may occasionally provide business or recreational entertainment or gifts of nominal value to employees and financial advisors.

Ameriprise Financial Services may, from time to time, offer contests, incentive programs, premiums or promotions to individual financial advisors or groups of financial advisors in particular areas. These programs may provide cash and/or non-cash compensation to financial advisors for sales of particular products or services.

From <u>BBVA Compass Bank</u>:

Possible Conflicts of Interests: BBVA's wide range of simultaneous activities in the field of Securities Markets, as well as the different family, economic and professional or other connections of Involved Persons make it possible that, at certain times, the following Conflict of Interests may occur:

5.2.1 Between customers of the BBVA Group.

5.2.2 Between customers and the BBVA Group.

5.2.3 Between different areas of the BBVA Group.

5.3 Specific cases of Conflict of Interests: Identifying a Conflict of Interests entails at a minimum, determining whether the BBVA Group or its Involved Persons fall within one of the following situations:

5.3.1 The entity or the person in question may obtain a financial benefit, or avoid a financial loss, at the expense of the customer.

5.3.2 Has an interest in the outcome of the service provided or transaction carried out to the customer's account other than the interest the customer has in said outcome.

5.3.3 Has financial or any other type of incentives that favor the interests of customers other than those of the customer in question.

5.3.4 The professional activity is identical to that of the customer.

5.3.5 Receives or will receive, from a third person an incentive in connection with the serviced rendered to the customer, in cash, goods or services, other than the usual commission or fee for the service in question.

This from <u>Bank of America</u>:

Conflicts of interest may occur when:

- *Personal interests or activities compete or interfere — or even appear to compete or interfere — with your obligations to the corporation, its shareholders or customers.*
- *The interests of two or more of the corporation's customers conflict, potentially giving rise to a material risk of damage to the interest of one or both of the customers.*
- *The corporation places its interests over the interests of its customers, without legitimate reason.*

<u>Edward Jones</u>

Edward Jones told the public and its clients that it was promoting the sale of the Preferred Families' mutual funds because of the funds' long-term investment objectives and performance. At the same time, Edward Jones failed to disclose that it received tens of millions of dollars from the Preferred Families each year, on top of commissions and other fees, for selling their mutual funds. Edward Jones also failed to disclose that such payments were a material factor, among others, in becoming and remaining an Edward Jones Preferred Family[6].

After the above enforcement proceeding findings, the following disclosures appear on Edward Jones website:

Revenue sharing, as received by Edward Jones, involves a payment from a mutual fund company's adviser [sic] or distributor, a 529 plan program manager, an insurance company or the entity that markets an insurance contract, or a retirement plan provider. It is not an additional charge to you. These payments are in addition to standard sales loads, annual sales fees, expense reimbursements, sub-transfer agent fees...

We want you to understand that Edward Jones' receipt of revenue sharing payments creates a potential conflict of interest in the form of an additional financial incentive and financial benefit

---

[6] SEC Press Release 12/22/2004

to the firm, its financial advisors and equity owners in connection with the sale of products from these product partners.

Genworth Financial

A potential for certain conflicts exists between the interests of contract owners and owners of variable life insurance policies issued by us or owners of variable life insurance policies or variable annuity contracts issued by other insurance companies who may invest in the Total Return Fund. A potential for certain conflicts would also exist between the interests of any of these investors and participants in a qualified pension or retirement plan that might invest in the Total Return Fund. To the extent that such classes of investors are invested in the Total Return Fund when a conflict of interest arises that might involve the Fund, one or more such classes of investors could be disadvantaged. GE Investments Funds, Inc. currently does not foresee any such disadvantage to owners. Nonetheless, the Board of Directors of GE Investments Funds, Inc. monitors the Total Return Fund for the existence of any irreconcilable material conflicts of interest. If such a conflict affecting contract owners is determined to exist, we will, to the extent reasonably practicable, take such action as is necessary to remedy or eliminate the conflict. If such a conflict were to occur, the Subaccount might be required to withdraw its investment in the Total Return Fund and substitute shares of a different mutual fund. This might force the Total Return Fund to sell its portfolio securities at a disadvantageous price.

From H.D. Vest

Securities offered through H.D. Vest Investment Services^{SM}, Member: SIPC (The unmistakable mark of a salesperson; not a true advisor/fiduciary).

This from Lincoln Financial Advisors:

In some cases, planners receive more compensation when placing Lincoln Financial Group manufactured products, and may qualify for additional compensation based on the volume of those sales over time. Conversely, because of the way products are priced, LFA planners may also receive higher compensation from companies not affiliated with Lincoln Financial Group.

In addition, some experienced new planners transitioning their practices to LFA have been offered loans in anticipation of future sales of Lincoln Financial Group products, and to a lesser extent, non-Lincoln Financial Group products. The repayment of these loans may be wholly or partially waived based on the attainment of certain sales levels or may be funded by additional compensation for these sales.

LFA affiliated companies may also benefit financially from the sale of proprietary life insurance, annuity, mutual fund and asset management products offered by our planners.

Here is a disclosure from a private investment planner:

At [small company] Investment Planning, Inc, we strive to provide to you with objective investment advice to assist you in retiring well. There are inherent in any recommendations, however, the potential for conflicts of interest. This conflict can come from the compensation our Financial Representatives ("FRs") may receive on specific investments or advisory services, or it may come from the compensation that [small company] may receive from third party providers as a result of your purchase of products, advisory or retirement plan services. It is important for you to understand these conflicts of interest so that you may make an informed decision to permit [small company] to serve your investment needs. (I thought they were being paid for their expertise to counsel about these decisions – here they say I'm on my own??)

From LPL Financial:

Conflicts of Interest, Sponsorship Programs: At LPL Financial LLC ("LPL Financial"), we receive compensation from the mutual fund families, variable and group annuity issuers and retirement plan product sponsors that are available to our brokerage customers.

From Northwestern Mutual

Depending on the products and/or services being recommended or considered, refer to the appropriate disclosure brochure for important information on the Northwestern Mutual Wealth Management Company, its services, fees and conflicts of interest before investing or engaging in financial planning services. To obtain a copy of one or more of these brochures, contact your representative.

Here is Pacific Life

It's My Responsibility to ensure that my personal interests do not conflict or appear to conflict with my business responsibilities. In any business transaction, I will place the Company's interest ahead of any personal interest or personal gain (to me or someone I have a close personal relationship with) and disclose all facts in any situation where a conflict of interest may arise.

From the Principle Financial Annuity Prospectus (957 Pages)

If you purchase shares of the Portfolio through an Insurer or other financial intermediary, the Portfolio and its related companies may pay the intermediary for the sale of Portfolio shares and related services. These payments may create a conflict of interest by influencing the Insurer or other financial intermediary and your salesperson to recommend the Portfolio over another investment. Ask your sales person or visit your financial intermediary's website for more information.

...the interests of various contract owners participating in the fund might, at some time, be in conflict due to future differences in tax treatment of variable products or other considerations.

The Fund or its distributor (and related companies) may pay broker/dealers or other financial intermediaries (such as banks and insurance companies, or their related companies) for the sale and retention of variable contracts which offer Fund shares and/or for other services. These payments may create a conflict of interest for a financial intermediary, or be a factor in the insurance company's decision to include the Fund as an investment option in its variable contract.

These payments may create a conflict of interest by influencing the insurance company and your sales person to recommend the Fund over another investment.

Prudential

Do not allow your personal interests (including investments, business dealings or other personal or family activities) to conflict or appear to conflict with the interests of Prudential, its shareholders or [lastly] customers.

Raymond James

The Company expects the undivided loyalty of its Associates in the conduct of Company business. It is important that Associates be free from any financial interests or other relationships that might conflict with the best interests of the Company and/or cloud their judgment in carrying out the business affairs of the Company. A 'conflict of interest' exists when a person's personal or professional interest is adverse to, or may appear to be adverse to, the interests of the Company.

UBS

We owe a duty to UBS to advance its legitimate interests. We must consult line managers or Legal & Compliance if our own interests either, actually or potentially, interfere or might appear to interfere with UBS's interests.

Wells Fargo Advisors

From time to time, Wells Fargo Advisors initiates incentive programs for all its team members, including Financial Advisors. These programs include, but are not limited to, the following: programs that compensate associates for attracting new assets and clients to Wells Fargo Advisors or referring business to its affiliates (such as referrals for mortgages, trusts or insurance products); programs that reward associates for promoting investment advisory services; preparing Envision® investor reviews; participating in advanced training; improving client service; and programs that reward Financial Advisors who meet total production criteria.

Financial Advisors who participate in these incentive programs may be rewarded with cash and/or non-cash compensation, such as deferred compensation, bonuses, training symposiums and recognition trips. Portions of these programs may be subsidized by external vendors and Wells Fargo Advisors affiliates, such as mutual fund companies, insurance carriers or money managers. Therefore, Financial Advisors and other associates have financial incentives to recommend the programs and services included in these firm-sponsored incentive programs rather than other available products and services offered by Wells Fargo Advisors.

Here is the point to close this chapter: These matters are complicated, especially the investment products which are not in your best interests. Investing successfully is about selecting the right people, who have your interests as their first priority, and who will direct you properly. You've learned a lot about what such a person "looks like," but there is still more to learn.

Chapter 6 - What Do All the Initials Mean?

"The expectations of life depend upon diligence; the mechanic that would perfect his work must first sharpen his tools."
    - Confucius

Put rather bluntly, I don't know what all the initials stand for, but I have a really good idea what they all mean. There are some primary designations in the financial industry. What I mean by primary is these require rigorous academic work AND practical experience in the substantive elements of financial advice. Here these are in no particular order.

CFP®

These letters stand for Certified Financial Planner®. This designation is the most widely recognized of all relating to financial matters. This wide recognition is due to the marketing efforts primarily of the Financial Planning Association or FPA, a trade organization comprised largely of those who have been granted the right to use the CFP® trademark.

The education component required for this designation is very good, but there is a better designation from an education standpoint. The due diligence effort which is exerted by the Certified Financial Planner Board of Standards before conferring the CFP® is without peer. What this means is someone who is a Certified Financial Planner® professional has been thoroughly vetted before that designation was awarded. Moreover, the Board of Standards requires ongoing compliance to maintain the use of its trademark.

My personal past experience is the Board is stringent but fair. Someone properly earning and maintaining their status as a CFP® professional has been knowingly approved and is being monitored. Nothing provides an error-proof stamp of approval, including the CFP®, but it does mean whatever history the advisor may have has been carefully investigated. It also means the individual has a significant level of competence, based on the education and experience required. It does not, however, distinguish between advisor and salesperson.

ChFC

This is the Chartered Financial Consultant, and it is the most rigorous education program available for financial planners. It is not as effectively marketed as the prior mark, and it has been largely defined by others as being strictly insurance-based. This is not the case. I have completed both of these designations personally and, when I did so, the ChFC was the only one to offer education on securities analysis – a substantial part of any good education related to investments.

ChFC does a superior job of teaching how to implement a financial and investment plan. The plan is certainly important, but the implementation is where the results come from. Any executive or business owner recognizes this reality.

CLU

This stands for Chartered Life Underwriter, and it is exclusively about life insurance. Given the role life insurance plays in most every financial plan, knowing the law, the products, and the implementation is extremely important given the gravity of most situations when life insurance comes into play.

The ChFC and the CLU programs are administered by the American College of Financial Service Professionals, an offshoot of the prestigious Wharton School of Finance associated with Pennsylvania University.

CFA

Chartered Financial Analyst. This designation deals exclusively with investments. It is difficult to earn, but coveted by mutual fund managers and other intermediaries. It has a strong due diligence component. However, when I examined the curriculum for the program it has as its foundation, almost exclusively, the tenets of MPT or Modern Portfolio Theory we discussed earlier. Not all of the world's best investment managers have this designation, at least in part, for the reason relating to MPT.

J.D.

This is an attorney. You need a will. In most states you need a trust. If you have minor children you need to name a guardian. If you have a business with other partners/shareholders you need a buy/sell agreement. The more substantial the dollars, and the more complex the situation, the greater your need for an attorney to assist you in these matters.

CPA

This is a certified public accountant. CPAs used to do taxes and financial statements only. However, over the last twenty years many accountants have embraced the idea of providing consulting services. As this has occurred, the line between fiduciary and salesperson have become blurry, akin to the financial advisor/annuity salesperson discussion we had in a previous chapter.

It is important to understand the things which make for a good accountant are very different from what makes for good investment results. An accountant is trained to track a trail of paper and/or cash and properly report its placements and usages. A good investment advisor is expected to take large amounts for disparate information including, but not limited to, the accountant's reports, and draw conclusions about the totality of the information to generate a profitable investment proposition.

Final Analysis

It is very important to understand and keep in mind each of these designations has certain strengths and certain weaknesses. None of them, standing alone, is either a foolproof way of determining the quality of the advisor, or of the advice. On the other hand, each is an excellent indicator of a substantial level of education and of meaningful vetting.

I know lots of nice people who have earned each of these designations whom I would gladly have dinner with. Moreover, I would trust most of them to formulate a financial plan for me and my family. However, none of these speak to the quality and efficacy of the advice you will receive nor to what kind of investment results will be produced. As we have said repeatedly in this book, it's your investment results which will have the greatest impact on your financial future. These designations speak volumes about a person's character and financial-related education, but say nothing about sound strategy and meaningful investment production. In a later chapter, I'll teach you concrete ways to evaluate this most important matter.

Chapter 7 - Understand Who the Regulators Are

"Under capitalism each individual engages in economic planning."
  - George Reisman

One of the great challenges of any society is monitoring and regulating professions. Doctors, lawyers, engineers, financial advisors, and others work on complex matters with advancing technology, multiple parties having (or seeking) an interest, and all occurring in an increasingly intricate legal environment.

In each profession, "someone" must establish, administer, and monitor licensing standards. In other words, there must be some sort of an agency which makes certain each candidate earns and maintains the necessary educational and professional basics to offer services. These administrators are frequently called "Self Regulatory Organizations" (SRO). The fact these entities exist certainly seems reasonable; even appropriate.

The challenge comes in, and this is a battle which has been fought in the medical profession for the last twenty years or more, when the law is involved. The agencies which administer and grant licensing are not law enforcement. They have no power to set the law, no power to enforce the law, and no power to punish those who break the law. The powers SROs have are to enforce membership rules and, where there is a breach of membership rules, they have the power to fine, suspend, or expel members. Certainly one of the rules can be no egregious law violations, but this is not a fail-safe as we shall see.

This is the reality of the financial services industry. There is an SRO named FINRA (Financial Industry Regulatory Authority), formally called the NASD (National Association of Securities Dealers). When you read what the letters FINRA stand for strictly at face value, it gives the impression this agency is THE regulatory agency for the financial business – but this simply is not true.

The only people FINRA currently "regulates" are in one segment of the financial landscape – a group of salespeople called stock and mutual fund brokers (individuals) and broker/dealers (firms). FINRA has no jurisdiction over the insurance sales people and none over true investment advisors. As a result FINRA (Financial Industry Regulatory Authority) gives the impression it is far more than an SRO (Self Regulatory Agency) when, in reality, it is not.

Earlier this year [2011], the Financial Industry Regulatory Authority (FINRA) made some noise about its desire to take charge of oversight and enforcement of investment advisers, a financial sector currently under the watchful eye of the Securities and Exchange Commission. The SEC must not have thought much of that proposal, because on Thursday the agency accused FINRA of altering documents and ordered the organization "to hire an independent consultant and undertake other remedial measures to improve its policies,

procedures, and training for producing documents during SEC inspections."

According to a statement from the SEC, "certain documents requested by the SEC's Chicago Regional Office during an inspection were altered just hours before FINRA's Kansas City District Office provided them." The charge focuses on three sets of minutes from August 2008 FINRA staff meetings in Kansas City, which are part of a larger set of documents the self-regulatory organization is required by law to submit to the SEC.

The SEC went on to note that this was not the first instance of a similar issue with FINRA documents: "According to the SEC's order, the production of the altered documents by the Kansas City District Office was the third instance during an eight-year period in which an employee of FINRA or its predecessor (National Association of Securities Dealers) provided altered or misleading documents to the SEC."[7]

The situation where there is an SRO presents two significant challenges. <u>First</u>, it provides the public with a false sense of security about the level of protection which is actually provided to investors. Here are some examples:

As I was researching this book, I ran a FINRA check on Allen Stanford, the Houston man reported to have bilked his clients out of an estimated $6 billion. At the time I looked, November 23, 2011, there was no entry of any kind for Robert Allen Stanford. In other words, if you went to FINRA and looked up the regulatory history of an alleged multiple felon accused of stealing billions of dollars from his clients, you would find nothing to indicate investing with him was even a questionable, much less a bad, idea.

When you look at the FINRA regulatory history of Bernard Madoff before his conviction on multiple financial felonies, there is not one single thing to suggest anything untoward. In other words, there was absolutely nothing in the records of FINRA to protect a prospective investor from the man who perpetrated the largest non-governmental Ponzi scheme ever. To the contrary, Madoff, was an industry darling – an industry many, incorrectly, believe is regulated by FINRA.

<u>Second</u>, a member can be expelled without breaking the law, without harming, or even impacting, any clients, and with very little recourse. I know this reality first hand.

In 1986, twenty-six (26) years ago as I write, I had a dispute with an NASD member firm over the requirement to reimburse that firm for costs they incurred while "training" me (You may recall my mentioning this in the prologue – the training I received was "how to cold call and give investors the pitch each profit center of the firm had given to "trainees" (there was no guidance about what to use and why, just sell).

---

[7] Corporate Counsel, ALM Properties, Inc. Brian Glaser 10/28/2011

Moreover, agreements such as this, where employment is conditioned upon accepting the agreement, are a violation of state law. As a result of my "violation" I was expelled from the NASD. When you look up my regulatory history, it gives the impression I have committed a heinous crime when, in reality, I was "kicked out of club membership" for erroneous reasons. Interesting, isn't it? For more than 20 years I have had this alleged "blemish" on my record, and two men who cost investors billions and billions of dollars didn't even show up on purported regulatory radar.

The only means FINRA provides for rectifying my situation is for me to leave my business as a true financial advisor and seek membership in its club as a financial salesperson. Thanks, but no thanks. In all my years in the industry I have no client complaints, no other issues related to clients or anyone else, and no true *regulatory* run-ins.

True Regulatory Agencies

There are agencies with real regulatory power. The Securities Exchange Commission (SEC), the State Securities Board of each state, and the various state insurance commissioners are the real watchdogs. But the fact these agencies exist does not mean the job is easy or air-tight protection for investors.

I have a relative who is a physician at The Mayo Clinic in Rochester Minnesota. When you go to Mayo's website, on a prominent page it says all people employed at the clinic have the primary responsibility of securing "the best interests of the patient". Everyone I have encountered at Mayo has taken this position in principle...and in practice.

Nevertheless, the specifics of healthcare law make it perfectly legal to do something other than that which is in the patient's best interest. There is no legal prohibition against giving chemotherapy to a 95 year old who isn't going to recover from pancreatic cancer (one of the most deadly forms of cancer). One could make the case in this specific circumstance putting a person through the agony of the treatment is pointless and, therefore, not in the patient's best interests – but it's still legal. In a situation such as this, when the law allows, but best interest doesn't, it is likely up to the patient and trusted family members to stop such a treatment. Remember this, because it is important in the financial context also.

Similar conundrums exist in the financial business. Regulators are harnessed by this reality in that they only have jurisdiction over what is legal and what is not legal. Said another way, regulators can only inspect "legality" and little or nothing else. It's perfectly legal to smoke cigarettes...overeat (my own particular weakness)...cheat on your wife or husband; but being legal doesn't make any of it a good idea. Regulators don't get to deal in "whether or not it's a good idea."

Before someone writes a book like this, those things which are legal but not a good idea seldom, if ever, make it onto the general public's radar. We saw concrete examples of this in the earlier section on "detrimental disclosures." An insurance company selling variable annuities and the like discloses the fact neither it nor its agent is acting in a fiduciary capacity. Purchasers sign off on this disclosure (at least implicitly). When an investor then tries to sue after she has purchased something which is not a good idea and not in her best interests, but is perfectly legal, she is thwarted by the law instead of protected by it. The same things happen to regulators who truly want to protect investors.

Regulators, whether medical or financial, have no authority to craft new laws of any kind, and certainly not ones that are situation specific. The simple reality is no one, even those possessing the authority to do so, can pass a set of laws which protect the best interests of all people, at all times, and in every situation. There aren't enough pages of print available to address all the variables and vagaries of each possible situation. This dramatically elevates the importance of your doing your own due diligence on the investment people you engage or employ.

While we have been laying the groundwork so far, in a later chapter I'll show you how understanding Stanford's and Madoff's business models would have protected your money against these people even though regulatory agencies weren't able to do so.

Chapter 8 - How to Achieve Excellent Investment Results?

"It isn't what we don't know that gives us trouble; it's what we know that ain't so."
  - Will Rogers

"Conventional wisdom is generally very bad wisdom when it comes to investing."
  - Martin Whitman

In the first two paragraphs in the chapter on the cause of investment losses are two critical statements: "…the thing which impacts your financial future to a greater degree than anything else are your investment results." "Far more money is lost due to false assumptions [and] counter-productive investment strategy … than from malfeasance."

Many investors fail or experience tremendous missed opportunity because of what they have been taught (or the things on which their financial advisors are basing their decisions and advice) about investing puts them in a position where the battle is lost before it ever gets started. "Conventional wisdom" today is all based on MPT (Modern Portfolio Theory) and, as we have seen, this approach is the complete epitome of "what we know that ain't so." This explains why so many people have been so badly harmed in each of the serious financial events over the last ten years.

What's interesting is the principles which will produce investment success are much simpler and easier to understand than what produces failure. The challenge is these successful principles are more difficult to implement consistently. It is this reason which prompts so many financial advisors to gravitate to MPT – it's easy for them to implement.

Combine this with the fact financial salespeople get paid primarily at the beginning of the investment process, and the investors' poor results sometime in the future don't (ever) meaningfully impact most advisors' financial situations. Their job is always finding new money. They are paid to bring in new funds. In their compensation structure, and consequently in their minds, the job of worrying about the investment results is someone else's responsibility.

The problem occurs because the client expects the person who sold the client the investments to protect the client interests. The advisor told the client in the beginning that avoiding losses was the purpose of MPT. When MPT substantially breaks down like it did in 2008, and investors loose gobs (a very technical term) of money, MPTs heretofore hidden, substantial, serious flaws are exposed. As I've said many times, if your investments are destroyed, what does it matter if what wiped you out was a once-in-a-lifetime event? <u>A fiduciary's responsibility, first and foremost, is the return of your overall capital, and after that, to earn a return on your capital.</u>

Now, having laid sufficient groundwork explaining what is wrong with much of the investment business, let's spend the rest of the book learning what you have to do to enjoy investment success going forward.

Sound Financial Principles and Practices

While most people cannot effectively manage their own investments, everyone who has ever bought groceries can understand sound financial principles. This is critically important as you evaluate the claims of prospective investment advisors.

Suppose you are cooking a nice dinner for six people on Saturday evening. You have not announced the menu in advance. Moreover, what you serve is not really a concern so long as the food is excellent. On Saturday morning you head to your favorite grocery store. You know the store typically has a special item on sale in each department. You've decided to walk the entire store identifying all the sale items. After doing so, you'll select the best-priced, best-quality, complimentary, menu items.

This brief story illustrates sound investment principles and practices. On any one day the specific investments are not terribly important. What every smart investment manager is seeking are high quality investments available at prices less than normal. Whether you're buying groceries or making investments, these are called bargains.

When grocery shopping we look to get more value than we pay for. High quality New York Strip steaks selling for $10.99 per pound when the regular price is $15.99 a pound, provide an opportunity to get more value than normal. Every day, we look to do the exact same thing in the investment business; that is, seek more value than what we pay for. The one difference between grocery shopping and the investment business is on most days I go looking for investments but I don't buy anything.

This is the approach of the world's most successful investors regardless of time period. All the names you have heard like Buffett, Templeton, Einhorn, Whitman, and so on follow this investment strategy. They each do so because this strategy produces consistently superior results with reduced real risk and good cash flow. <u>These three things: consistently good results, reduced risk and cash flow are the linchpins of investment success.</u>

Like most people who come to my office, you're probably saying this makes sense. You are also saying "That is so simple." Both are true and, as I suggested to you earlier, sound investment principles are simple, but it's the implementation which proves quite difficult. THIS is the reason you need to hire investment counsel. Throughout the rest of this chapter are more specifics about sound investment principles. With this information you are well-prepared to meaningfully interview and question potential advisors.

Timing and Selection

MPT says the specific investments you make and when you make them doesn't matter. Try telling this to someone who bought an expensive house via a big mortgage with no money down in August of 2008. Television and newspapers have done numerous stories on these people who owe far more on the mortgage than the house is now worth. *Timing and selection matter on everything you buy, and this is doubly true about investments.*

A high quality investment made at the wrong time (wrong price) is far more likely to turn out to be a bad investment. A low quality investment made at the right time may work out alright. But a high quality investment made at approximately the right time (right price) will prove to be an exceptional investment. This is what successful investors look to do.

The diagnostic is this: if you ask your (prospective) investment advisor about timing and selection and they respond, "It doesn't matter," Run!

Investment Prices

Every business day between the hours of 9:30 a.m. and 4:00 p.m. Eastern Time, someone is willing to make you an offer to buy or sell almost any possible investment. These are the hours the U.S. investment markets are open. Let's call this group of buyers and sellers by the name "Mr. Market." Some days Mr. Market is rather optimistic, on other days very pessimistic and on still other days, quite realistic.

If you had to associate Mr. Market with a personality, he would be a teenager. Some days Mr. Market doesn't care what happens, he is just excited and happy. Other days, even if he won the lottery, he'd be miserable. But most days he is pretty normal. Most people want to be around teenagers on the good days and avoid them on the bad days.

Most investors behave the exact same way. People make investments on days when everyone is happy as indicated by the markets and prices going up. They sell investments when everyone is miserable and prices are falling. This is the exact opposite of what one must do to be successful investing. We'll explain this in more detail in the next chapter.

Change in Investment Prices

Unsuccessful investors view *changes in the price of investments* as very negative. We call this change in prices "volatility." If you think about it, in order for an investment to make money, the price must change and there must be price volatility. If the price stays the same, little or no money is made. If the price goes up after you make the investment, then you make money. If the price goes down after you make the investment, then you potentially loose money.

MPT seeks to eliminate price changes and volatility as a means of reducing risk. October 1987, March 2000, and the fourth quarter of 2008 all proved it is impossible to eliminate price volatility. An investor can no more keep prices from changing, sometimes quite rapidly, than a beach front property owner can prevent waves from crashing onto the shore. Both the property owner and the investor must adapt themselves to the conditions because no one single person has the power to change the market or the ocean.

In order to be successful either place, one seeks to anticipate the conditions ahead and prepare for them. The beach front owner cannot build a retaining wall in the middle of a storm. He must build when the conditions are calm and hospitable. The investor must buy when everyone else thinks the world is ending and sell when everyone is convinced the streets will soon be paved with gold. Warren Buffett says he is "greedy when everyone else is fearful and fearful when everyone else is greedy."

Because most investors make decisions like the teenager above, the price changes they experience generally work against them. This is because they have invested when prices are rising and, understandably, the next price move is down. If investors made their selections to buy when the teenager is miserable (fearful) and their selections to sell when he is giddy (greedy), then price fluctuations would generally work for them instead of against them. This is a difficult thing to do and the reason people 1) stop investing, 2) buy expensive insurance products, or 3) hire a qualified investment advisor.

Understand Investment Risk

As we have mentioned before, MPT views price volatility as risk, and the only measure of risk. As we have shown repeatedly in the preceding chapters this is nonsense. On top of just being flat out false, risk cannot be so simplistically viewed, understood, or characterized. As I think about it, this is partially true. One certainly can view risk in this simplistic fashion, but it results in substantial failure as we have seen before.

Risk is not a constant and, as a result, it cannot be a single variable. Risk is ever-changing. Let me see if I can illustrate this. Suppose you have a 40 foot pleasure boat on a lake someplace in the United States. Perhaps the boat is on a Corps of Engineers lake in the Southwest. Maybe it is on one of the Great Lakes in the Midwest. Or maybe in Puget Sound in the Northwest.

Regardless, when the boat is moored in the harbor it is at risk from other boats entering and exiting boat slips immediately around it. If left sitting in the water too long, it is at risk for the hull delaminating or bubbling and springing a leak.

As you leave the slip the risks change. Because few harbors are of uniform depth, there is risk of running aground. Because there are docks, rocks, and so on, there is risk of running into obstacles in the immediate vicinity. As you get into open water, the risks again change. There is the risk of large floating objects submerged just below the waterline. When the boat is moving slowly there is maneuverability risk. When the speed increases it takes longer to come to a complete stop. When the number of other boats in proximity to your boat increases, risk increases. When the speed changes in other boats, risk also changes. If the boat captain is intoxicated the risk increases. If other boat captains are intoxicated, risk increases dramatically. What about darkness, wind, tides, current, and rough water? Each addition, subtraction, or alteration of a risk issue changes the risks which must be addressed. So it is with investing.

Moreover, if the boater concerns himself with only a single risk, such as shallow water, he fails to put lights on the vessel because he doesn't pay any attention to the risk presented by darkness. Any knowledgeable boater considers leaving lights off a boat to be preposterous, and so it is. Having no boat lights is obviously a ticket for disaster, as is an investment approach which concerns itself with only price volatility.

Investment risks include interest rate risk, market risk, credit risk, timing risk, operational risk, financing risk, and so on. These risks occur at various times in varying degrees. If you hire an investment manager, or a boat captain with a myopic view of risk, you're going to end up in the cold, dark water. Your investment advisor needs to understand these different risks while employing strategy and tactics to deal with them *before the storm starts*.

Critical Importance of Cash Flow

The average investor, one who is not a business owner, receives automatic cash flow management during their working life. We call it a paycheck. Every week, every two weeks, or perhaps every month, an employee receives a paycheck from his employer. With each check some is paid to taxes, some is saved and invested, and some is spent. Each additional paycheck brings an inflow of cash. The only management required is to make sure one spends less than one brings in.

When living off of investments, cash flow production and management is absolutely critical. This is because one must time the payment of expenses with cash produced from investments. If one has lots of assets but runs out of cash, then investments have to be sold to produce cash. If the markets are very pessimistic, selling assets to raise cash can result in huge investment losses. Losses like this can badly damage an investment portfolio in a way that one can never recover.

Before retirement, producing investment cash flow provides new funds to invest in bargain investments. After retirement, having sufficient cash balances and cash inflows protects against losses due to poorly-timed selling.

Transparency

This will seem obvious, but regardless of who is managing your money, you need to know exactly what you own. You'll likely own some stocks, bonds, cash, and real estate in some form or fashion and you want to know specifically which stocks, bonds, cash, and real estate it is.

You want your advisor to buy publicly and directly-traded investments. This makes things easy to track and report. One of the problems with mutual funds and annuities is it can be very difficult to get timely transparent information and reporting.

A second concern is mutual funds and equity-related annuities are non-transparent ways to own investments. Both vehicles give investors a completely accurate picture of what is owned at only four instants in time: the end of each quarter. What is owned the rest of the entire year is shrouded in varying degrees of mystery. Not knowing the specific investments limits profit potential and risk reduction options. It increases the likelihood that investments will be sold at a loss when cash must be raised.

All sorts of worse things can take place in situations where transparency is compromised or eliminated. <u>You can avoid much of this risk by simply insisting that an independently-produced, continuous record of specific portfolio assets be available to you at all times. This is a very simple service to provide and there is almost no situation wherein you should compromise on this point.</u>

In this chapter, we've discussed investment risk concepts and principles. To ignore these sound investment principles is to lose the battle before it even begins. In the next chapter we'll talk in more detail about the benefits of approaching investing from this foundation.

Chapter 9 - Benefits of Sound Investment Strategy

"Buy when others are despondently selling and sell when others are avidly buying... [This]
pays the greatest ultimate rewards."
>   *- Sir John Templeton*

Timing and Selection

The point of all investment is to generate the greatest of *ultimate* rewards. Great rewards won't be generated in a day, a week, or a month. Even if rewards were generated this quickly, the taxes would eat those rewards alive. Successful investing is very much like farming. At the right time and under the right conditions, crops are planted. Then, those crops are tended until the crops indicate they are ready to be harvested.

When it comes to investing, the right time to "plant" is when everyone else is afraid and despondently selling. The last time despondent selling took place was in November of 2008 and March of 2009. Strong selling pressure also occurred late in the summer of 2010. When there is despondent selling, there are far more sellers than buyers. It looks something like this:

Sellers: ¶   ¶   ¶   ¶   ¶   ¶   ¶   ¶

Buyers: ¶   ¶

When it comes to buying or selling, you get the best deal if you are one of the few doing it. The reasoning is pretty simple. In the example below, there are eight buyers and two sellers. There are four times more people seeking to acquire an investment than the number of people seeking to unload that same investment. In some sense, each of the eight buyers is competing against each other for the right to make the purchase. It's a bit of a crude illustration, but this is similar to early morning shoppers lining up outside an electronics store three days before Black Friday sales take place. Although the prices are set by the store, people do all kinds of things to make sure they get their desired item.

Buyers: ¶   ¶   ¶   ¶   ¶   ¶   ¶   ¶

Sellers: ¶   ¶

When it comes to investing, the large number of buyers is not limited to a fixed price like the buyers at the electronics store. When there are a larger number of "avid" buyers the price can, and does, go up. If you are selling an investment when most everyone else wants to buy that investment, the increasing price produces a substantial benefit to the prospective seller. The better news is avid buying usually occurs late in the cycle, meaning significant rate of return probably has been earned by the investor who put money in when everyone else was despondently selling.

Investment Prices

Over time, investment prices will equal the value of the company. But there are times when the price and the value are two very distinct numbers. Let's suppose an auto dealership owns five brand new $50,000 cars and nothing else. For some reason the owner of the dealership has decided to sell the business and needs to accomplish the sale in a hurry. He is asking $175,000 for the dealership. For the person who has cash and can wait for a period of time to sell the cars, a potential profit of $75,000 is available.

In this case, the price is $175,000 and the value is somewhere right around $250,000. If the owner was not in a hurry he could patiently wait for the cars to sell and pocket the full value of $250,000. Because of his haste, there is a $75,000 difference between the price and the value.

Understand Investment Risk

When an investment advisor can buy a quality asset at a bargain or sale price, there is great potential for profit and there is a reduced risk. In the extreme, the investor can only lose $175,000 if he buys the dealership and gets absolutely nothing for it. This is a reduced risk compared to the person who buys the dealership for $250,000. The purchaser at $175,000 gets the same amount of assets for less money when compared to a buyer at $250,000. Smart buying of quality investments at reduced or bargain prices, is an outstanding way to increase return and reduce risk.

Critical Importance of Cash Flow

Now, let's suppose that the dealership pays a dividend to its owner. The annual dividend is $10,000. At a price of $250,000, the $10,000 dividend equates to a 4% annual yield. But when purchased for $175,000, the $10,000 dividend amounts to a yield of 5.7%. What's more, this higher yield comes at a reduced risk.

What most people do when relying on their investments to produce income is "chase yield." This is the practice of making risky or substandard investments because the interest or dividend received is high. Many investments with high yields are weak and pathetic investments, which carry more risk. Locating high quality investments with good dividend yields are available, but harder to find. Nevertheless, locating the latter produces better cash flow with lower risk. Whether you are a retired investor living on cash flow or someone still building assets who reinvests cash flow, better yield at lower risk is a good thing.

Transparency

Knowing what you own is one of your best resources in times of trouble. Below is a table of the profitable stocks we owned in the depth of the financial meltdown in the 4th quarter of 2008. Our clients owned the following six stocks, which all had profits based on our purchase price and the market closing price on 10/8/2008.

Investment Name	Buy Date	Buy $	Melt Price	Melt Date	Gain	Growth
Amgen	3/28/2008	$41.56	$52.12	10/8/2008	$10.56	25.41%
Genentech	12/6/2007	$65.78	$80.56	10/8/2008	$14.78	22.47%
Covidien	12/6/2007	$40.54	$47.75	10/8/2008	$7.21	17.78%
Johnson & Johnson	2/12/2002	$57.05	$62.36	10/8/2008	$5.31	9.31%
Proctor & Gamble	6/30/2008	$60.58	$66.10	10/8/2008	$5.52	9.11%
Oracle	2/12/2007	$16.61	$16.88	10/8/2008	$0.27	1.63%

First, if we had invested clients' funds in mutual funds or equity based annuities we would have no idea what, if any, investment was profitable.

Second, because these six investments were worth more than what we paid, if a client needed emergency cash in the middle of the financial crisis, we could have gotten that cash without incurring a permanent loss of capital. The problem created by owning mutual funds is being forced to sell at a price less than what you invested. To be fair, our clients owned other investments also, which if we had been forced to sell would have generated losses. But having these six companies where we knew profits existed protected all concerned against having to sell other things at a loss.

Third, several of the companies paid dividends during the crisis, which could be distributed or reinvested at the appropriate time. It was transparency in part (because we knew what was owned and which investments owned were profitable), which made all of these very valuable benefits possible in the depth of the financial crisis. Further, it was good timing and selection of investments which put our clients in a position to be profitable in these investments during that very difficult time.

Conventional Financial Practices of Little Value

Let's briefly discuss two practices of little or no value. These are dividend reinvestment and dollar cost averaging.

It is an excellent idea to invest in things which pay dividends. It is also a great idea to reinvest those dividends. The problem comes in when one uses something called *automatic dividend reinvestment*. With this tactic, instead of receiving dividends in cash, any time dividends are paid the investor receives dividends in the form of additional shares.

The actual mechanics of this arrangement are not usually apparent to the investor. When dividends are automatically reinvested in additional shares, the cash dividend that the investor would have received is used to *purchase* additional shares at the market price on the day the dividend is paid. At the bottom of the cycle, when share prices are cheap compared to value, this is fine. But at the top of the cycle, the dividends purchase shares that are more expensive than the value. Simply allowing dividends, interest, and other cash earned to accumulate allows the advisor to invest funds at times and in things which are priced cheaply relative to value.

Dollar cost averaging is a process where equal dollar amounts are invested across specific time intervals, typically monthly or quarterly. In this arrangement, the calendar determines the timing of purchase rather than the price-to-value relationship of the investment. This same problem exists in automatic dividend reinvestment programs; the calendar dictates instead of price-to-value. The relationship of price-to-value is always the more important determinant because it has the greater effect on, and greater potential for, positive results and returns.

Making investments according to these two tactics is purported to increase returns and reduce risk. But, as someone who personally administered and invested 401(k) plans for more than ten years, I can tell you neither approach produces either increased return or reduced risk over long periods of time when compared to investing according to the price-to-value ratio (A 401(k) plan is the ultimate example of dollar cost averaging as money is received and investments are made at the same time each and every month).

Widely Used High Risk Strategies (You should avoid)

Momentum investing is buying an investment because it has already gone up in price. The expectation is whatever has gone up is going to continue to go up. This approach requires a certain amount of arrogance because, to be successful, it requires selling the investment to an even more gullible person. Seldom does this happen. Frequently, the pitch accompanying momentum investing is "this time things are different." Reality is the foundational principles of successful investing never change. Momentum investing was very much in vogue during the technology bubble, which occurred in 1998 and 1999.

High Yield Bonds are also known as junk bonds and are of lower quality than investment grade. A less-than-investment grade bond is a speculative bond. In the beginning of this book, I mentioned working for Drexel Burnham before I started my own company. Drexel Burnham was the originator of the "junk bond." Michael Milken did research which found junk bonds had default rates lower than expected and that smart investors could make an additional "free" rate of return by investing in them.

At the time Milken did his research, the only junk bonds available were formerly investment-grade rated bonds which had fallen in quality and value for some reason. It seems reasonable a company, which at one time was investment grade, could "rehab" itself and return its bonds to this level of quality. But a "fallen" bond is very different from a bond rated junk (below investment grade) when it comes to market. Bonds which are issued as junk bonds have lesser quality finances and businesses. In the 25 years I have been gone from Drexel, I don't recall a bond issued as junk becoming and maintaining status as investment grade. The reason for this is when the company becomes investment grade, it buys back the junk bonds and borrows money at the lower rates higher quality borrowers receive.

Buying a high quality company with no regard for price is a very risky strategy. As we said earlier in this book, buying a quality company at too high a price turns a great investment into a lousy one.

It is important, when interviewing investment advisors, that you listen for these telltale signs of risky investment practices. You should also continue to listen for these troublesome strategies throughout your relationship.

Chapter 10 - Who Can Productively Put Your Money To Work?

Productivity is never an accident. It is always the result of a commitment to excellence, intelligent planning, and focused effort.
- Paul J. Meyer

There is a perception the financial business is sexy and exciting. To embrace or subscribe to this notion is a mistake with long lasting implications. Successful investing is painstaking, disciplined work. There is a mountain of material to read every day. There is research to do. Every truly successful investment advisor either does their own research or seeks to independently verify the research done by others. This is not the stuff of super-models.

When you see Warren Buffett, Bill Gross, David Einhorn, Kyle Bass, or Harry Markopolos in the media, the first thing that comes to your mind is not flaunted, flashy sex appeal. What comes to mind when you see and hear these men is hard working, diligent, and relentless.

Money (capital) is a tool to the successful investment advisor. It's not her god, it is her servant. No responsible employer disregards or disrespects an excellent employee. But neither does a responsible employer allow an employee to lever or manipulate them. Money as a tool or employee is powerful. Money as a god is cruel and heartless. Money as a tool improves conditions. Money as a god destroys everything and everyone around it.

There is an old adage that goes something like this: "What you worship is what you become." Well, there is a corollary in the financial business and it is: "What you think you own ends up owning you." Every truly successful financial manager I have ever encountered, including me, takes the position he is a steward of whatever is entrusted to them. This is not only the productive but also the correct mindset to have, for it is definition of a fiduciary.

The <u>first</u> thing you're looking for in an investment advisor is a mindset like a secret service agent. It's the job of the secret service to protect the president. They secure the area, they seek to anticipate what can go wrong, they want to direct him to safe and productive areas, and they put the interests of the president ahead of their own. This is the thinking and these are the actions of an investment fiduciary.

The <u>second</u> thing you're looking for is an arrangement where your interests and the interests of the advisor are aligned. Airline pilots are a great example here. Everyone on an airplane has interests that are aligned. Everyone wants to take off on time, do so safely, arrive in one piece at the destination on schedule, and make their way quickly home or to their loved ones. Hijackings create problems because the interests of the passengers and the interests of the operators conflict. Need I say more?

<u>In the investment business, aligned interests have the advisor and the investor benefiting at the same time, by the same events/occurrences/decisions, and in the same proportion. A financial</u>

salesperson makes money in spite of the client and well in advance of the client doing so (if ever). A fiduciary makes more money as the client's investment increases and makes less money as the client's account decreases. This happens all at the same time and in the same proportion for both parties.

The third thing you are looking for is someone to grow your capital, rather than just moving money around. I recently purchased a car. It was the debut model of a hybrid sedan, and when it came out I wasn't really looking to buy a car. As a result, it took three visits to the dealership over two or three weeks to get everything completed. On each trip, I noticed the cars on the dealer's lot were in different places. One week the SUVs were here and the next they were over there. Evidently there is a full time person who "re-merchandises" the vehicles each week. This person may not sell cars. He may not service cars. He may not repair cars. This guy just moves cars around for a living.

In the auto dealership or department store, this makes complete sense. The retailer wants people to see and fall in love with his merchandise. The more varieties of merchandise he exposes people to, the greater the likelihood someone will fall in love with something he sells. But in the financial business, just moving money around harms the customer and only enriches the salesperson (and maybe the IRS). You're seeking someone to deploy your capital productively and leave it there until it is time to harvest. When a successful harvest has occurred, at the right time capital is redeployed.

Understand there are perfectly respectable, upstanding, well-meaning people of integrity who are asset gatherers and not productive money managers. If you are looking to have your money warehoused, perhaps this is a reasonable way to do it. But with inflation, taxes, and the various other ways capital is eroded, what you need is someone to deploy your resources productively, not simply store them. Knowing how to set up an account from tax perspective or expertly affecting transactions does not mean the "advisor" knows how to deploy capital productively.

The fourth attribute of the person you're looking for is someone who, more often than not, anticipates what is going to happen and deploys your capital accordingly. One of the things I noticed in early 2009 was advertisements for "safe" certificates of deposit. Perhaps this sounds reasonable because interest rates would soon fall. But, buying CDs in the first quarter 2009 was doing so after the market had already fallen. If one was going to buy CDs, it would have really helped to *anticipate* and have done so during the summer of 2008. This would have preserved funds by selling high and earning interest as the market fell. Buying a CD in 2009 was doing so *after the fact*.

In broad terms, anticipating what is going to happen is accomplished by someone with experience. I personally have been in the investment business during October 1987 when the market crashed 25% in less than a week, through the recession in the early 1990s, through the market meltdown when Long Term Capital Management failed in the late 1990s, the tech bubble, the run-up to Y2K, the real estate bubble, the sub prime meltdown, the recession that followed and now the European Debt Crisis. I used to hear people say they put their money with some "young go-getter". I even talked to a man at the meat market one day who said he selected his financial advisor based on how "hot she was." Funny, I never see him buying steaks anymore.

Productively deploying capital requires diligent research and accurate analysis. Here again, there is no sex appeal, just plain old hard work. The big brokerage firms will talk about their research and analysis capabilities yada, yada, yada. What I find interesting is the one who does the research at those firms is not the one who must deal with the clients and vice versa. In my firm, and other successful firms, these two functions are inexorably intertwined. It's that way with Bass, Einhorn, Buffett, and Gross.

Anticipating what comes next is not something even great investment people do with extreme precision. Great hockey goalies have save percentages close to 97%, meaning they fail only three percent of the time. Great investment managers don't have anywhere near the success rate. But the good news is that a ridiculously high success rate is not required to productively deploy capital and reap substantial rewards as a result.

Successful investing requires both timing and selection. To deny this reality is to be absolutely wrong before even a single dollar is invested. Denying these requirements assures failure. The wildly successful need only be approximately right to produce great results for customers. Whereas false notions of investing (MPT) break down under extreme conditions, the soundness of selection and timing shines during these periods. In these cases the investment advisor need only be approximately right to produce substantial returns, reduced risk and protected capital. It is far, far better to be approximately right instead of absolutely wrong.

How do you find such a person?

This is an excellent question. We'll talk more about this in the next chapter where I describe what a productive investment management relationship looks like.

Chapter 11 - Productive Management Agreements/Engagements

"Patience and Diligence, like faith, remove mountains." - William Penn

The first "screen" is to avoid people whose business cards say, "Securities offered by...Member SIPC." This brief statement on the card indicates the advisor generates commissions from transactions. This arrangement contributes to his income simply by his moving money around. Regardless of the advisor, this is a compromise which works against your interests through higher commissions and hedged income. The true fiduciary benefits at the same time and proportion as you do. Earning commissions on the transaction means the salesperson is earning money without regard for the investor.

No Salespeople

You want a financial advisor who actually manages money. Buying mutual funds, ETFs (exchange-traded funds) or annuities is not managing money. Some "advisors" charge an assets-under-management fee for selling you these products. This process is not management of assets. It is the sale of products with an expensive fee added on top. Only pay asset management fees to someone who is actually managing your assets.

No Surrender Charges

Whatever you invest in should have no impediments to leaving. Now, this is not possible in every single investment situation. But, even good hedge funds provide opportunities for clients to remove as much money as they want at certain times of the year. When there is a surrender charge for exiting an investment, it is an indication at some level that prior investors wanted to get out of the investment – because the surrender charge exists to impede or prevent exit or sale from happening.

Forfeiting interest on a CD because of early withdrawal makes sense. The bank seeks to match borrowers' loan terms with depositors' investment duration. Even in this case, there is no impediment to leaving; there is only an interest forfeiture. Certain mutual funds, and almost all insurance-based investments have lengthy and, sometimes severe, penalties for exiting. You'll be trapped by these in ways you don't want and at times which compromise your investment results. Make sure you can leave if, and approximately when, you want to.

This next paragraph is the most important in the entire book

You want an advisor whose business model leaves him no choice but to do what is in your best interests and do it very well. In my firm, we receive no investment income of any kind, except that which we bill our client's investment accounts. We receive no commissions, 12b-1 fees, incentive payments, soft dollar benefits, bonuses, sales awards, sponsorships, office subsidies, "free" research or services, or any other inducement when it comes to managing and advising our customers' investments.

The only money we earn is what we bill on a fully disclosed basis, each and every time we bill. It is very easy for our clients to determine they are getting great results vis-à-vis what they are paying. If they believe they are not getting value, there are no impediments to exiting our service offerings at any time.

There are good people who operate in other business models, but they have choices which potentially compromise investors. There are many operating in these other business models who are about advancing themselves and not about protecting your interests. This is how you recognize and avoid them.

LPOA

The engagement between you and a qualified investment advisor (DO not use this with a financial salesperson) should be a limited power of attorney (LPOA). This agreement provides limited powers for your investment advisor to effectively manage your funds. There are three basic parts to this agreement:

1) The advisor is authorized to make investments on your behalf.
2) The advisor is authorized to receive duplicate trade confirmations and account statements.
3) The advisor is authorized to bill your account for the management fee.

These three things are the only powers needed for a qualified investment advisor to manage your investments for you.

Fees

Pay management fees only to someone who is actually managing your assets. If you buy ETFs, mutual funds, or get referred to a "professional money manager," those folks are the ones managing your money – do not pay management fees to anyone else (especially the person who referred you to these managers). Who is deciding the specific stocks, bonds, real estate, etc. you are investing in? Pay management fees to them and only to them.

Discretion

Most qualified investment advisors are going to manage your money on a discretionary basis or not at all. This means the manager decides in what, how much, and when to invest. So long as he or she abides by the other principles in this book, this should not be an issue. It is these essential elements of investment management you want someone to perform for you. Just make sure the great bulk of your capital is invested directly in stocks, bonds, cash, real estate and NOT in mutual funds, ETFs or other non-transparent vehicles.

Disclosures

Every investment advisor operating properly must provide you with an ADV form disclosure. It is imperative that you read this. In it is all the information about the advisor, which allows you to evaluate him or her against the criteria we have laid out for you in this book. This generally is not as long as a prospectus and should be in easy-to-read language. A thick, legalese document is a red flag, but is not automatically a deal-breaker. As I said, though, it is a very large and conspicuous red flag.

Chapter 12 - Annuities and Insurance as Investments

Either you repeat the same conventional doctrines everybody is saying, or else you say something true. It will sound like it's from Neptune.
     - Noam Chomsky

Current conventional wisdom on insurance-based investments has two tenants. The first tenet is: "Equity based insurance investments give you all of the return of the market with none of the risk." And the other tenet is, "Any insurance-based investment is a rip-off." Here is the truth: and even though it may sound like it, this is not from Neptune!

We'll deal with the former first. Craig McCann, an attorney and investment specialist, has said it best.

"Annuities [and variable insurance investment products] are costly, complex investments sold based on typically insignificant tax or insurance benefits by financial advisors with strong financial incentives adverse to those of their customers. These financial advisors receive generous commissions for selling annuities to investors who would be far better served by investments in individual stocks and bonds or mutual funds."[8]

"...in most situations, investors being sold annuities [and variable insurance investment products] will pay more taxes and have less wealth in retirement as a result of the tax treatment of investments within tax-deferred annuities. We also report the results of scientific literature which demonstrates that the death benefit feature [of annuities] is worth a tiny fraction of what insurance companies charge investors for this feature.

"Given their tax disadvantages, illiquidity and trivial insurance benefits, the phenomenal growth in the sales of annuities can only be attributed to the powerful incentives offered to salesmen and the industry's obfuscation of the true costs and benefits of annuities."

"The added expense associated with the variable annuities that are the subject of this article cannot be justified unless the annuity is held for an extended period of time—perhaps for decades, as our analysis will show. It follows that variable annuities should not be sold to individuals who are retired or close to retirement. Yet a great many variable annuities are sold to these individuals. Given the limited period of deferral, there is no reasonable prospect for the tax deferral benefit to outweigh the costs."

"Annuities are sold as tax advantaged products. Whether the sales force describes annuities as tax advantaged or tax deferred, the sales pitch is materially false for the vast majority of annuity purchasers."

---

[8] Annuities by Craig J. McCann, PhD, CFA and Kaye A. Thomas

"For many years we have had favorable rates for long-term capital gain, and more recently the same favorable rates apply to qualified dividend income. Annuities do not preserve the benefit of these lower rates. On the contrary, they convert capital gain and qualified dividend income into ordinary income that is taxed at higher rates."

"Annuities stand out as the investment most likely to be unsuitable since in virtually every instance, the investor would have been better served by mutual fund or a portfolio of individual stocks. That variable annuities hold more than $1 trillion in assets is a testament to the powerful incentives created by the insurance industry with generous commissions and the massive fraud they engender."

"Insurance companies add trivial insurance benefits, disadvantageous tax treatment and exorbitant costs to mutual funds and sell them as variable annuities."

"We estimate that between 15% and 20% of the [money invested] by investors in equity-indexed annuities is a transfer of wealth from unsophisticated investors to insurance companies and their sales forces."[9]

Well, that will just about take care of "equity based insurance investments give you all of the return of the market with none of the risk."

Limited Window

There is a very limited number of cases where expecting insurance to pay off as an investment is a plausible idea, and only one or two where it will truly be a good idea. Here are the plausible ones:

1. Those who cannot save without being "forced" to do so (by getting a billing or having an automatic withdrawal from checking account).
2. Those who cannot leave money without having a penalty to prevent early withdrawal.

Even these folks should almost never use variable or equity-related annuities and insurance due to costs of the contract and all other reasons mentioned above. I say "almost never" even though I don't know, and can't presently think, of a single situation when these are appropriate.

When Combining Insurance and Investment Pays Off

Up until the Mid-1980s, what you're about to read wasn't the case. Things do change and things have changed in what I'm going to share with you. Straight, bland, non-sexy, universal life and whole life insurance have many of the benefits of bond funds without the drawbacks.

In the first quarter of 2012 as I write this, interest rates are basically zero. Savings and checking accounts pay little or no interest, even for a whole year. CDs, municipal bonds, government

---

[9] An Overview of Equity-Indexed Annuities By Craig McCann, PhD and Dengpan Luo, PhD

bonds, and even corporate bonds do not pay enough interest to offset the risk of owning such things.

But, at some time, interest rates will rise. When this takes place, the value of the bonds you currently own, or purchase, in this low interest rate environment will fall. In other words, your principal will decline in value unless you hold every bond to maturity and none of them defaults.

With boring, standard, old life insurance cash values, this reduction of principal does not happen. In fact, when interest rates rise, the rate of return on the cash in the insurance increases. This is not the case with bonds. The bond principal declines in value, and the bond interest payments remain the same when interest rates rise. The cash value of a life insurance policy doesn't decline when rates rise, AND the interest paid on cash increases when this happens (Equity and variable based insurance products DO NOT benefit from rate increases).

Moreover, quality insurance policies have a contractual floor for interest earnings. This means the amount of interest the insurance company pays to you cannot fall below the floor. Four or five years ago, we recommended that our clients who needed life insurance consider this sort of cash value policy. Those who took our advice have been getting four percent interest even as interest rates have gone to zero. Those contracts have an interest rate floor of four percent. When interest rates rise, the earnings already received are protected against interest rate risk (principal reductions), and the rate of interest will increase as overall interest rates increase.

The tax consequences are ultimately the same as bonds, with the exception that the ongoing interest receipts from insurance are tax deferred until a withdrawal (a better deal than bonds). Also, the fees and expenses with this kind of insurance are much more easily identified. Don't do this strictly as a cash-on-cash investment. But if you need regular life insurance, this can be a very effective strategy for money you would otherwise place in bonds.

There are two types of insurance companies: one you should avoid and one you should use. A stock insurance company is one owned by shareholders and is almost always traded on the stock market. Shareholders want higher premiums because this benefits shareholders of the company. Shareholders want lower payouts and interest crediting because this benefits the shareholders of the company.

A mutual insurance company is owned by the policy owners, in other words, those who have insurance with the company. The policyholders want low premiums, low expenses, and high interest crediting/payouts to owners of life insurance. The stock company has an inherent conflict of interest between insurance customers and those who own the company. A good mutual company has no such conflicts. So, if you need life insurance and need a place to put bond money in a low interest rate environment, buy cash value life insurance from a well-rated mutual life insurance company.

This case and the one prior, where someone cannot save money on his own, are the only cases where mixing insurance and investment makes sense.

Chapter 13 - Your Single Greatest Protection Against Malfeasance

"The truth is incontrovertible. Malice may attack it, ignorance may deride it, but in the end, there it is."
- Winston Churchill

If you recall from Chapter Three, "far more money is lost due to false assumptions, counter-productive investment strategy, "professional" inexperience, misplaced focus, impatience, ineptitude, and herd mentality, all combined with the investor's misunderstanding of the financial services delivery system, than from malfeasance." For this reason, we have focused all of the attention in the book thus far on these larger issues. You are far more likely to lose money over these than because of fraud.

Nevertheless, some people do lose money to fraud and malfeasance. These stories never have happy endings. I pay careful attention to these cases when they go public because I am looking for the tipping point: that point in time where the situation could still play out either way. Without exception, the tipping point is the beginning of the formal relationship between the fraudulent operator and the investor.

This is the time when the investor signs an investment management agreement and writes a check. Without exception, the name you write on the check is the <u>first step</u> in protecting you from every investment con game and/or Ponzi scheme I have ever heard about or researched.

If you make the check out to anyone other than a completely independent custodian, you are at risk. Independent custodians operating today are national discount brokers, such as TD Ameritrade, Fidelity, and Charles Schwab. These three firms, and probably a handful of others, offer custodial services for independent investment advisors like the ones we have talked through and recommended in this book.

The rules concerning investment advisor custody of assets have become more stringent since the Madoff revelations. But even these new rules have weaknesses. Your best protection, whether engaging an investment advisor or investing in a hedge fund, is to place your funds only with a qualified, independent custodian. If the advisor operates in any arrangement different from this, don't invest. Having your funds held by an independent custodian is simple and free. Combine this with the second step, and it's the best protection you'll ever have.

The <u>second step</u> is to make sure the money remains in your name. This is accomplished by having the investment advisor establish accounts in your name at the discount broker/custodian. You can compromise the benefits of the independent custodian if you put money in the investment advisor's name or firm name.

When someone places IRA money with my firm for management, we establish the "George Washington" Individual Retirement Account. The money remains in George's name held in custody at an independent custodian. We manage George's money under the terms of the LPOA we discussed earlier. It doesn't matter what type of account "George" wants managed, his funds always stay in his name. This is the second leg of protecting your funds from malfeasance. Keep them in your name at an independent discount broker.

Among custodians, TD Ameritrade and Shareholder Services Group currently provide additional protection to investors based on services each firm *does not* provide. This has become more important as a result of the Jon Corzine and MF Global situation. These firms don't do research, have no proprietary investment products, and neither does investment banking or trade for its own account. Because these firms do not offer or engage in these other things, client funds are not at risk from the firm trading activities, as was obviously the case with MF Global.

Ponzi Scheme Characteristics

It is estimated investors lost about $25 billion of cash in the Madoff scheme. Alan Stanford is reported to have bilked investors out of about $6 billion. This is real money. You obviously want to avoid this problem. Here are characteristics these schemes have in common:

- *Guaranteed returns or promised returns higher than market interest rates.* Any time you are guaranteed a rate of return, it is an indication the money you are investing is being loaned to someone. Certificates of deposit promise a guaranteed rate of return because the bank is loaning the money to a borrower. The bank pays investors less interest than it charges the borrowers. Therefore, a higher than market rate of interest suggests one of two things, and each is bad: 1) the borrower is a high risk borrower, thus the higher interest rate for the loan, or 2) the promised return is, at a minimum questionable and, at the maximum, completely bogus.

- *Returns which are above market and incredibly consistent from year to year.* This result is highly desirable but completely unrealistic. The very best investment managers do not produce eleven percent (11%) returns each and every year. They may *average* eleven percent (11%) return on an annual basis *over time*, but extremely consistent high annual returns are a tip off.

- *Lack of accountability, lack of independent verification, and/or statements.* When your money is managed by an investment advisor under an LPOA (Limited Power of Attorney) and held at an independent custodian, the independent custodian sends you monthly statements of your account. The investment manager can do nothing to alter or interfere with these statements, as long as they come directly from the custodian. Madoff "created" and sent out his own statements. Therein lies the problem (pun intended).

- *Lavish and conspicuous spending on high-end lifestyle.* Certainly the range of what people consider lavish has a wide band. Some consider driving a Lexus lavish and conspicuous spending, while others see this as value-oriented transportation. Madoff and other schemers made a point of using their spending to draw attention to themselves – expensive homes, yachts, and all made quite publicly. By contrast, Buffett, Gates, and Einhorn, while certainly having nice things, use their spending to benefit others or to put capital they have earned back to work.

- *The size of the financial advisor does not matter*. Madoff had a very substantial organization, as did Stanford. McLean in Tennessee had an organization of only one or two people. When it comes to con schemes, size truly does not matter.

- *Requesting trust instead of common sense*. In all my years in business, I have never asked a client to trust me. My approach is to build credibility and explain things in a way that is understood. We ask our clients to make an affirmative decision to go forward based on an understanding of what I have explained. In all investment-related questions I can think of, "trust me" is not an acceptable answer.

- *Inability or refusal to explain the investment strategy (perhaps for proprietary reasons)*. There are very few, if there are even any, proprietary strategies when it comes to investing less than $25 million of a client's resources. What sets investment advisors apart is an ability to judge, decide and execute. Just because someone is told how a particular approach works doesn't mean even a small percentage of people can replicate it. I have no qualms of any kind about explaining how we manage money because the strategy we follow still must be executed.

Chapter 14 - Check Out Your (Potential) Advisor

Whatever you do, you need courage. Whatever course you decide upon, there is always someone to tell you that you are wrong. There are always difficulties arising that tempt you to believe your critics are right. To map out a course of action and follow it to an end requires some of the same courage that a soldier needs. Peace has its victories, but it takes brave men and women to win them.
- Ralph Waldo Emerson

Quite clearly, when it takes more than a dozen explanatory chapters to lay the groundwork for checking out your advisor, we're talking about a complex subject. There aren't three easy rules to "eternally protect your money." It seems most people today, me included, want simple, easy, linear answers to difficult questions and situations. When it comes to due diligence on the productive investment of your capital, there isn't such a thing.

Thinking there is a simple set of fail-safes will have you eliminating some highly qualified advisors, while walking straight into the arms of the wolf (in sheep's clothing). This calls for some behind-the-scenes work before you ever hear any presentations or ask any questions.

If you recall, data provided by FINRA relates primarily to whether the advisor in question has violated any of the club's rules. It also contains law violations, but there is no bright line between the two types of issues. You must dig through this information to determine if a problem really exists and what the true nature of the problem is. If there are client-related issues, such as "unsuitable investments" or "customer complaints," there is cause for concern.

This is further complicated by the fact that FINRA is responsible for operating the Broker Check website and data distribution. You also need to be aware Broker Check currently discloses issues only when the individual or firm has three or more regulatory actions or historic complaints. This makes a thorough vetting on Broker Check somewhat nebulous at best to just about worthless in the worst case.

Additional Data for More Thorough Vetting

Someone who has the CFP® (Certified Financial Planner) or CFA® (Chartered Financial Analyst) certifications has been thoroughly vetted. These are not the good housekeeping seal of approval of their business models and practices. But, these people are likely to be people of integrity because of thorough vetting. Again, this is no fail-safe, but it is another indicator. You can search CFP records at http://www.cfp.net/find/EnhancedSearch.aspx.

CFA Institute's professional conduct page is
http://www.cfainstitute.org/ethics/conduct/Pages/index.aspx

You can also search these sites by advisor name for issues and concerns. http://dockets.justia.com/ Court dockets and filings

http://www.pacer.gov/ Public Access to electronic court records
http://www.finra.org/Investors/ToolsCalculators/BrokerCheck/index.htm Broker Check
http://www.naic.org/state_web_map.htm Respective state securities commissioners.

Epilogue

"Even if you're on the right track, you'll get run over if you just sit there."
  - Will Rogers

It's pretty clear the SRO pseudo regulators are not going to protect you and your investments. Here are the questions the actual regulators suggest you ask of prospective investment advisors:

1. **What experience do you have, especially with people in my circumstances?**
2. **Where did you go to school? What is your recent employment history?**
3. **What licenses do you hold? Are you registered with the SEC, a state or the NASD?**
4. **What products and services do you offer?**
5. **Can you only recommend a limited number of products or services to me? If so, why?**
6. **How are you paid for your services? What is your usual hourly rate, flat fee or commission?**
7. **Have you ever been disciplined by any government regulator for unethical or improper conduct or been sued by a client who was not happy with the work you did?**

These are legitimate questions, but in no way will the answers you are provided protect you or your money. The logical conclusion is that none of the actual or quasi-regulatory agencies are going to protect your money. This job falls to you and you alone.

The answers to all of the questions above are included in the advisor's ADV form. If you recall, I said very explicitly that you must read this document. All investment advisors must provide it. Financial salespeople have no such requirement. This fact alone is a way to discriminate between someone you should consider retaining and someone you should not.

So, the first thing you're going to do in your personal due diligence is check out the advisor information and background at the websites specified in the preceding chapter while making notes of any areas of concern or in need of additional questions/further clarification.

Next, you are going to read the advisor's complete ADV form, again making any relevant notes or questions.

Finally, you're going to schedule an interview and ask these questions in your meeting with the advisor:

1. **Explain items or questions of concern (you uncovered in your own investigation – chapter 15) in checking out the advisor.**
3. **Who has custody of my funds? Whose name are the funds titled in?**
4. **What is the agreement between me and the custodian? Me and the advisor? Me and the person I am talking to?**

5. Who is making the investment decisions as the specific stocks, bonds, real estate, and cash I'm investing in?
6. What is your position on MPT and how do you implement it?
7. What is your position on making investments in/through insurance contracts?
8. What is your position on momentum investing?
9. How do you decide when to sell?
10. Put on one page for me the direct and indirect expenses I/my funds are paying (name all who are getting paid and how much)?
11. How do I make money? When do I make money? How much money do I make?
12. How do you get paid? When do you get paid? How much do you get paid? How will I know?
13. What incentive payments, inducements, or services in kind do you receive?
14. What is your plan for protecting me against losses?

If you diligently follow these steps in your investigation and qualification of investment advisors, you will uncover the substantial matters which contribute to or detract from the advisor's ability to productively put your funds to work.

If you have more than $500,000 of investable assets and want to discuss management from Dana's firm, call 972-231-4444 or email dana@thebarfieldgroup.com.

If you have additional questions you can e-mail Dana at dana@thebarfieldgroup.com. He answers these as his time permits.

About the Author

Dana Barfield, CFP®, ChFC, MSFS

Dana is the President of The Barfield Group, Inc, a Registered Investment Advisor. Barfield formed the company in April of 1990 after stints at large financial firms, including a multinational insurance company, an investment bank, an international brokerage firm, and a regional pension manager.

His name is most closely associated with doing that which is in the best interests of his clients. Barfield started the firm based on the idea he would neither retain the services offered, nor pay fees in the amounts charged, by most financial firms. Using his insider's knowledge of the financial business, he created a business model which delivers concrete benefits to clients, at a price and format for which he would be willing to pay. The result is an industry-leading firm with more than 21 years of experience and outstanding client benefits, delivered at a low cost. Clients are physicians, business owners, and those they refer.

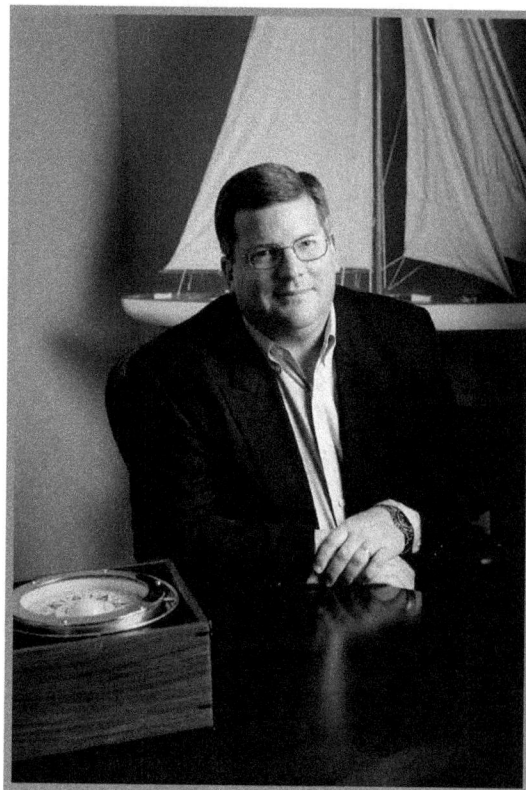

Barfield is a long-time critic of the way Wall Street, many insurance companies, and most financial firms do business: The way they establish and protect conflicts of interest with their customers, their practice of enriching themselves to their customer's detriment, for exploiting the public's expectation of expertise, and delivering a sales pitch for high priced products of nebulous investment value.

He holds a Master of Science in Financial Planning, is a Certified Financial Planning Professional (CFP), and a Chartered Financial Consultant (ChFC). These three degrees/designations represent the most comprehensive and rigorous financial education available.

Dana writes a syndicated financial column under the name of RetirementWhys.com, is the author of three books on finance/business ownership, and is a sought after speaker on financial, wealth generation, retention, and business ownership topics. He is the founder of a teaching ministry named Real2Ideal.

He lives in the Dallas, Texas area with his wife and daughter.

Index

www.ingramcontent.com/pod-product-compliance
Lightning Source LLC
Chambersburg PA
CBHW051228200326

41519CB00025B/7296